NOT ANOTHER GREEK SALAD

ANN RICKARD

NEW
HOLLAND

First published in Australia in 2004 by
New Holland Publishers (Australia) Pty Ltd
Sydney • Auckland • London • Cape Town

14 Aquatic Drive Frenchs Forest NSW 2086 Australia
218 Lake Road Northcote Auckland New Zealand
86 Edgware Road London W2 2EA United Kingdom
80 McKenzie Street Cape Town 8001 South Africa

National Library of Australia Cataloguing-in-Publication Data:

Rickard, Ann (Ann J.).
Not another Greek salad.

ISBN 1 74110 152 2.

1. Greece - Humor. 2. Greece - Description and travel. 3.
Greece - Anecdotes. I. Title.

914.95

Managing Editor: Monica Ban
Project Editor: Glenda Downing
Designer: Karlman Roper
Production Manager: Linda Bottari
Printed in Australia by McPherson's Printing Group, Victoria

10 9 8 7 6 5 4 3 2 1

CONTENTS

IN SEARCH
OF ENLIGHTENMENT
AND LESBIANS

Shortly after I'd written my first book, *Not Another Book About Italy*, I read *Dark Star Safari* by seasoned travel writer Paul Theroux, a story about his grand journey from Cairo to Cape Town. He wrote of dangerous experiences, thrilling encounters, ghastly sickness, arduous travel and filthy toilets. He was robbed and stranded in remote dusty villages; he interviewed government ministers in Zimbabwe; he hitched rides in rattly old cars crammed in with a dozen smelly people and assorted animals—all in order to bring you and me interesting travel tales. While he wrote about having to kill time and a chicken when stranded in yet another poor African village, I wrote about lazing in a deckchair and drinking Limoncello in enchanting Capri. While he wrote about the difficulties of dealing with corrupt border guards on the longest road in Africa, I wrote about the annoyance of having to pay to sit on a beach in glamorous Portofino.

'Call yourself a travel writer?' I said to myself because I was too embarrassed to say it to anyone else. 'You're a sham, a fake. What kind of serious travel writer bangs on and on about drinking copious quantities of wine in Siena? Stuffing herself with spaghetti in Sorrento? Shopping capriciously in Rome? Traipsing whimsically around Tuscany?'

The shame of it.

After Paul Theroux's trip to Africa, during which he ate something poisonous, he sat down to write his saga with 'Africa stirring inside me—the reminding motion and gassy gurgle of my parasites.'

After my trip to Italy, during which I ate and drank everything I came across from the top to the boot of the country, I sat down to write my story with Italy stirring inside me—the reminding motion and gassy gurgle of a warehouse of wine.

For a while after reading this book about Africa, I had writer's block. I knew I should be writing another travel book, for I had many more notes about my time spent in Italy. But I could not even look at my laptop, let alone sit down to it and actually turn it on. Every day I promised myself that this would be the day I'd start another book. But it never was. The laptop became a demon that taunted me every time I skirted around it, making me miserable with shame, tortured with guilt.

When you know you should be writing but are frightened to start, every other ordinary chore becomes important and interesting. Cleaning the toilet is a pleasure compared with the act of touching a computer keyboard. Even scraping six months' worth of gunk out of the dishwasher filter is an enjoyment when measured against the task of actually having to compose prose.

'I simply cannot call myself a proper travel writer,' I lamented to Geoffrey one day while rapturously scrubbing out the rubbish bin. Geoffrey is my husband, the man I wandered happily with that gorgeous summer in Italy and talked about a fair bit in *Not Another Book About Italy.*

'All I did was visit Italy with you and have a fabulous time and then write about it,' I said. 'I should be more adventurous, go some place dangerous so I can write like other travel writers. I haven't been shot at, robbed, ridden in a cattle truck, been stuck in a remote Africa village, or faced a horrible toilet—apart from our own before I started cleaning it so enthusiastically.'

'Do you actually want to be robbed and shot at?' Geoffrey asked, looking understandably anxious. 'If you're really serious, we could go to Africa. We'll go if you honestly think you should be writing about stuff like that.'

I gave this some serious thought for a whole minute.

'Maybe,' I said. 'But the Greek islands sound good.'

So it is off to Greece we go, in search of inspiration and lesbians. The lesbians are to come by way of a month's stay on the island of Lesbos. Our research leads us to choose this island not because of the many smirking remarks we've heard about gay women visiting Lesbos, but because it appears to be one of the least commercial of the Greek islands. On Lesbos, a hotel room is a fraction of the cost of its counterpart in Santorini. Our guidebook tells us that Lesbos is an island which still has its natural charms, and a classical history dating back more than three thousand years. It is a place where many of Greece's most famous poets, musicians and philosophers lived; an island which was one of the great cultural centres of the ancient Greek world. Lesbos has a petrified forest, ancient ruins, a thriving agricultural industry, pretty fishing harbours, unspoilt villages and culturally enlightening museums. But we do hope to see lesbians. I can't deny that.

We will also stay for a few weeks on Sifnos, another island that the guidebook promises has not been spoilt by tourism, has a long and rich history and is home to more than four hundred churches and monasteries. We also want to visit Athens again for a few days, and hop around the other islands, as whim and our budget will take us.

We have been to Greece and the Greek islands more than once before. Our most memorable Greek trip was the one we did on a motorbike in 1970, when we were living in the UK. We were young, newly married and in love, and actually enjoyed sleeping in each other's arms on an inflatable mattress in a tiny tent. It was a time when our backsides were firm enough to stand five uncomfortable hours a day on a hard motorbike seat, and when eating cold canned food by the side of the road and showering with dozens of others in communal facilities in camping grounds actually seemed like fun.

I delve into the musty pages of my 1970 diary to see what wonders of Greece I recorded. I look at the scrawly girlish handwriting, touch the yellowing pages and remember that splendid period of my life. My memory tells me we spent a good couple of months in Greece that summer, riding all over the mainland, making camp in small coastal towns, travelling on rusting ferries for trips to the islands, living gloriously happily and rampantly sexually in our tiny tent.

Even though I have braced myself for what I know are inadequate diary entries, I still manage to shock myself. One typical diary entry shows my lack of observance.

'Slept till 10 am. Drove down to a small place along the coast. Arrived around 2 pm. A very, very small place.'

Maybe I was so blinded by love and new marriage that I noticed nothing else but Geoffrey. Another diary entry reveals my adoration.

'Went to the bar in the campsite and watched Geoffrey drinking ouzo all evening. It was lovely.'

Watching Geoffrey drinking ouzo was lovely?

Oh dear. As fond as I still am of dear Geoffrey, spending an evening watching him drink ouzo now sounds about as exciting as cleaning out the dishwasher filter I just told you about.

One of the strongest memories I have of that 1970 summer in Greece is not of ancient ruins or fishing villages, or bouzouki halls, or the Acropolis, but of Geoffrey cracking one of the lenses in his glasses. He used to wear Coke-bottle glasses with thick black rims back then, and I think I accidentally sat on them one morning in our little tent. Naturally, we didn't have any spare money or travel insurance, so we stuck a bandaid over the crack until we could get back to the UK and the then excellent free health system. At about the same time a crown I had over a dead and shorn-off front tooth fell off. It was unthinkable that I should go to the expense of getting it repaired in Greece when it could be done for free back in the UK, so I stuck it back on, where-upon it immediately fell off again; and continued to do so for the rest of our travels. How we must have looked to the Greeks when we arrived in some new town or village—Geoffrey with his patched glasses, me with a stump of blackened front tooth—is beyond think-ing. No wonder so many locals seemed to shy away from us in shops and take startled steps back when we approached them at reception counters or asked for directions in the street.

Now, although we set off for Greece in 2003 amid fears of SARS and in the middle of a war in Iraq, we at least have contact lenses, attractive back-up glasses, travel insurance, and a set of Hollywood-style crowns that would make even Britney Spears envious. But people in shops and reception areas still shy away from us and take small steps back when we approach them and this puzzles us deeply until much later—almost at the end of our trip—when we are told unceremoniously that we are 'big and intimidating'. I'll tell you more about that later.

The first pleasant surprise on arrival in Athens is the gleaming new airport. This is as modern, as state-of-the-art and efficiently func-tional as an airport should be for a city just a year and a bit away from staging the Olympics.

The airport might be clean, spacious and efficient, but it doesn't offer a free trolley service. There are few things more annoying to jet-lagged travellers struggling to get large suitcases off the baggage carousel and juggling heavy hand luggage than trying to find a coin for a trolley when they haven't even had a chance to change money into the local currency. Actually there are more annoying things. Finding a taxi driver in Greece who doesn't smoke. In the oppressive Athens summer heat, a chain-smoking taxi driver in an un-airconditioned taxi is not a comfortable thing. But our dark and sweaty driver is at least pleasant, even though he makes no attempt to hide his amusement when we tell him our hotel is the Hotel Economy.

'Well, that says it all,' he says, obviously annoyed that he mistook us for the sort who would stay at the Athens Hilton and give big tips to taxi drivers.

'It was recommended,' I tell him and he grunts, lights another cigarette from the one he is about to throw out the window and speeds us along the impressive new motorway right into a gridlock on the outskirts of Athens. Everywhere there is the ugly chaos of work in progress. Athens looks like one giant building site. Signs tell us there are five hundred days until the Olympics, and instinct tells us it is not possible that everything will be finished in time. When you think that every time workmen in Athens start to build something, they come across some treasure of antiquity and have to stop work, it is understandable that things move a bit slowly. It is quite awesome to think that most new work in Athens ends up uncovering yet another archaeological site.

It is a Sunday afternoon, and yet the traffic is at standstill. Everywhere around us roads are torn up, tall cranes pierce the sky and heavy machinery sits empty.

'Greeks always leave things until the last minute,' our taxi driver says. 'Greek people don't stress about work. They will start in the morning, work for a few hours and then stop for coffee and cards, and by then it's too hot to start work again so they sit around for the rest of the day.

But the work will be finished for the Olympics, I suppose. Look at that,' he points to large piles of dirt by a wide trench in the middle of the road. 'They are building the metro right out to the airport and they are supposed to be working twenty-four hours a day to finish it.' There is not a workman in sight.

'We look forward to the Olympics finishing more than we do them starting,' he says and we all go quiet then, because we can see what a terrible mess the people of Athens are living with now.

It seems to take the entire afternoon to get into the heart of the city and we are all tetchy by the time we arrive. The driver gives another snort of disdain as he finally pulls up outside the doors of the Hotel Economy, behind the old town hall. He adds an extra 10 euros onto the 50 euro fare 'for the helpful tourism advice and conversation I gave you' and dumps us and our luggage on the footpath.

Still, we are pleased to have arrived here without shaking in fear, as we did on our arrival in Athens eight years previously.

For that holiday, we had paid in advance at home—$100 Australian, I remember the figure clearly—to have a driver waiting for us at the airport. We had not been back to Greece since 1970, and our travel agent had warned us that a transfer from the airport to our hotel would be essential: our flight landed at four-thirty in the morning, and a driver holding a sign with our name on it in the arrivals lounge would be a reassuring sight because taxis would be rare. And it would indeed have been reassuring—had the driver and his sign actually been there.

We waited patiently outside the terminal for twenty anxious minutes in the cool dark of the early morning, looking longingly at the line of taxis waiting to ferry everyone else into the city for about the equivalent of $15. Finally, when the entire planeload of people had gone their various ways into the dark and we were left alone at the now empty airport, we gave up hope and made our way to the taxi rank, mentally constructing a rude letter to the travel agent back home demanding our $100 back, when a young man suddenly appeared, running across the road, tucking his shirt into his pants and brandishing a sign with our name on it. He asked if we were the Rickards and we stupidly admitted that we were.

'You must come with me, you must,' he said pulling us away from the taxi rank and towards his own car. We were annoyed, because we had been about to save the pricey transfer fee, and went with him most reluctantly.

No apology was forthcoming, even though it was obvious that he had slept in and was unforgivably late. As he drove us through the sleeping Athens streets he sensed our anger, and did not like our refusal to be drawn into conversation. We should have known this was wrong of us. He became aggressive.

'Did you make your hotel booking starting from today or yesterday?' he asked nastily over his shoulder.

We were intimidated, and told him we were booked in from today.

'Then I will make sure you don't get into your room until this afternoon, at the check-in time of three,' he said. 'I don't like you. If I liked you I could have got you into your room right now, but now you must sit with your bags and wait until three o'clock this afternoon. You are not nice people. I don't help you.'

The little bastard. If he tried that on today I'd see to it that his boss realigned his testicles, but eight years ago we were just beginning to travel again after being bogged in Australian suburbia for decades, and we were not at all sure of ourselves.

We sat quietly in the back until we reached the hotel. He ran in to reception ahead of us, shouting angrily in his own language to a sleepy old man at the counter, obviously telling him not to give us our room until the official check-in time. The old man blinked rapidly and looked worriedly at us as the driver stormed out, bellowing and waving his arms angrily. We were told to sit on the chairs in the lobby (it was another hotel in the mode of the Hotel Economy, and the chairs were hard plastic) and wait.

It was the most miserable of arrivals in Greece for a holiday we had worked hard for and anticipated with so much excitement. We felt wretched and stupid.

It was still pitch dark outside, and deathly quiet—both on the streets and inside the hotel. Apart from the old man behind the counter, there was not a soul around. We had been travelling for about thirty hours from Australia and now faced almost an entire day's wait until we could check in.

After about an hour the old man either took pity on us or decided we had been punished enough—or, more likely, could not stand the sight of two scruffy, unhappy people loitering in his lobby any longer—and told us we could have our room. We were pathetic in our gratitude, even when he showed us to a room only slightly bigger than our kitchen pantry back in Australia.

We were so upset by the taxi driver, and so certain this was to be the way all Greeks would respond to us—even though we had nice glasses and good teeth now—that we opened our duty-free bottle of Southern Comfort. It was about six-thirty in the morning by this stage, and why we had bought Southern Comfort is still a mystery, because it is something neither of us—both known for our fondness for most types of alcoholic beverages—has ever touched. We sat on the small bed in the tiny room with our legs up under our chins and got stuck into the booze. We tried to analyse the taxi driver incident, at first reasonably and then drunkenly, wondering why he became so angry and malicious. We soon realised this was futile, and decided to explore the Acropolis instead. It was all of eight o'clock in the morning.

There was no-one collecting money at the Acropolis—actually there was no-one there at all—so we lurched up the steps and staggered blearily around the monument by ourselves. Geoffrey remembered how neglected and unpreserved the Acropolis had been back in 1970.

'Don't you remember how it was just crumbling and in ruins?' he said.

'Well it is a ruin, isn't it?' I slurred.

'You know what I mean,' he said. 'The Greeks didn't realise what an icon they had back then and hadn't done anything to maintain it or turn it into a tourist attraction. Don't you remember how neglected it was?'

Remembering was a bit much for me at eight-thirty in the morning with quarter of a bottle of Southern Comfort running through my veins. I did remember an old 1970 photo of me looking pretty spiffy standing in front of the Acropolis columns, but what I remembered most was the vivid pink mini sundress I was wearing. It had those cone-like breast things Madonna made famous, and my titties were poking out a couple of metres in front of me like witches' hats. Every time I look at that old photo I don't even see the stately Greek columns—all I see are hot pink cone boobs. But Geoffrey was determined to remember, and he made me scramble and trip around the Acropolis to look at the work being done to bring the monument back to its original glory. Some details I had studied in the past came back to me later, when the Southern Comfort fog cleared.

In the couple of thousand years since the Acropolis was built, it has been plundered by various invaders, and many of its artworks are now in other museums around the world. The Acropolis has been bombarded, besieged, set on fire, rocked by earthquakes, used as a Turkish mosque and a Christian church, and has had flags of the many invaders of Greece raised on it.

No wonder it had looked a bit tired in 1970.

I remember it being especially pleasant to have this wondrous place all to ourselves before the tour buses and flocks of people arrived. We explored it thoroughly in the quiet and cool of the morning and it was marvellous, even if we were too drunk to appreciate the finer nuances of its splendour. We came across a group of young soldiers on flag-hoisting duty in the far corner of the Acropolis. They were treating the small ceremony very seriously, and looked terrified as two big inebriated people approached them and tried to strike up a conversation. They politely answered our stupid questions for a few minutes and then quietly edged away to a safe distance, from where they ran away.

We wove our way back to our hotel for a much needed sleep, and later that afternoon, refreshed but still alcoholically poisoned, we wandered through the Plaka, a few minutes' walk from our hotel, and had a delightful lunch of Greek salad and fried fish in a charming restaurant beneath a trellis of flourishing grapevines. Feeling a little perkier, but still upset by the taxi driver incident, we arrived back at the hotel and found I had left my handbag, complete with passports, money and travellers cheques, in the restaurant. We ran back in a fine panic, to be greeted by the friendly owner, who had stored my bag safely behind the counter. He insisted that we check the contents to ensure that everything was intact before we left, which it was.

Our spirits soared. Our faith in the Greek people was instantly restored.

And we never again touched Southern Comfort.

Having got those memories out of the way, we tingle a little with excitement now at the thought of making a new lot of memories over the next couple of months, and after we check in to the Hotel Economy with a friendly bespectacled young man who could not be more obliging—and who is one of the few people we are to meet who does not take a step backwards when we approach him—we tell him briefly about that trip eight years ago. We had time then to visit only a few of the islands but loved them all, loved Greece, found the Greek people more than friendly. We knew it was going to be the same— even better, now. Here we are in Athens, the birthplace of European civilisation, and we can feel evidence of that all around us. We are right at the beginning of a long holiday in this sunny and most glorious of countries and there is much to anticipate. Most Greek people speak excellent English, which is just as well, as we speak no Greek at all. They are generous in their hospitality. They are honest. They are happy. They sing. They dance. They love eating. They love drinking (our kind of people). They are welcoming and embracing. They can fish. They can cook. They have a great sense of humour. They have fascinating art, thrilling museums, old amphitheatres galore, more icons than they know what to do with, one of the greatest histories in the world, and enough ancient ruins to share with everyone. They are great storytellers. They love life. They love Australians. Eight years ago we struck probably the only nasty taxi driver in all of Greece. And I'd tell you his name was George if only all the good taxi drivers in Greece weren't also called George.

ATHENS PREPARING FOR THE OLYMPICS

The Hotel Economy in Athinas Street, just minutes away from the Plaka and the Acropolis, turns out to be rather good even though it is right next door to the Silver Star Sex Shop. Small and recently refurbished, it is more than adequate for our needs (the hotel, not the sex shop), and taking the six flights of stairs to our room is easy compared with the idea of getting into the tiny lift that looks more like an upright coffin. After we settle in we take a short walk to the Plaka, the old town that winds around the base of the Acropolis and is a hive of daytime activity and bustling nightlife. It is 9 pm and still very hot as we walk across the near empty square outside our hotel. We pass a small group of men who appear to be on the verge of a vicious fistfight. About six of them push and shove at one man, and finally one of them hits him hard on the jaw. It makes an awful thwacking sound, which sickens me.

'Just ignore them and keep walking,' Geoffrey the Brave says while I whimper and try not to look at the ugly scene. Another of the men kicks the man violently in the groin and it looks certain that a terrible beating is about to take place.

'Perhaps we should interfere,' Geoffrey finally says, just as another group of tourists approaches and shouts at the men to stop. We quickly walk on and away from the nasty scene, but it leaves me feeling upset and disturbed.

I have a split personality when it comes to violence. I love nothing more than reading books about serial killers and I can easily read a Wilbur Smith where men have had their genitals cut off and shoved in their mouths before being nailed to trees, but put me near a real life man getting his jaw whacked and his crotch kicked, and my innards go all watery.

I will never understand myself.

From the town hall square, we make our way around the mess of roadworks, stepping around orange netting and picking our way over broken concrete until we come to the bright lights of the Plaka. At the base of the awesome structure of the Acropolis, the Plaka is a labyrinth of narrow streets, handsome churches and beautiful old homes. Throughout the exciting old quarters are lively cafés and tavernas, elegant restaurants and beckoning shops, all among the stateliness of the Byzantine churches and mosques. You can't help but love it.

We wander through the packed streets on this hot June night, wondering what it will be like in July and August, when the heat and tourists become more intense, more insane.

Some of the narrow pedestrianised streets are blocked completely by the spreading tables and chairs of the tavernas on either side, as proprietors bring more and more tables out to cope with the crowds. Pedestrians are forced to pick their way slowly through the packed tables.

It looks so enticing that we look around for an empty table ourselves. As soon as we stop, half a dozen waiters immediately pounce on us, bring out another table from inside, and miraculously find a small space for us, half on the footpath, half on the road. The wait staff dash through the maze of tables writing down orders on little notepads and shouting back into the kitchen at the same time, so that food appears almost before the orders have been recorded. Within one minute we are served eggplant dip, moussaka, a Greek salad and a basket of hard bread.

An old and authoritative-looking grandpa sits on a chair by the taverna door, watching everything with an observant eye. Judging by the way the staff keep respectfully and nervously glancing at him, he is the owner.

These tables must surely be turned over fifteen, twenty or more times a night. A cash register has been set up out in the street and it doesn't stop dinging for a minute.

'This place has been established since 1879,' Geoffrey says, reading from part of a sign he can see from his balanced position. 'Six generations offering the best food in Greece,' he says. We'll eat to that.

We have never seen so many people being served so efficiently.

'How many people would you serve here a night?' I ask our waiter as he runs past us.

'Hundreds and hundreds,' he boasts, stopping for just a moment. 'We have a staff of one hundred people working twenty-four hours a day during the busy season. I can easily retire for the winter.' And he runs off.

We eat our moussaka and watch the action. The tables are set with bright green cloths, and over the cloths are sheets of strong clear plastic held down just under the rim of the table with a thin piece of elastic. As people move away from their table after their meal, a small team of well-coordinated waiters swoops instantly, pulls up the four corners of the plastic, with all the dinner debris in it, and whisks it away while another team moves in behind them and lays another sheet of plastic over the table. This all takes about twenty seconds, and the table is ready for yet more customers. It is beautiful choreography, and as impressive a dining scene as I have ever seen—production on a grand and efficient scale. The food is obviously all pre-prepared, but it's good, and the street itself provides the ambience.

Three male musicians dressed in embroidered shirts and pantaloons wander through the mass playing Greek music, stopping at each table to play for a few minutes. The guitarist has a small basket hanging from the end of the guitar neck, and after each chorus, he dips his guitar so the basket—his tip basket, we now see—is right under noses. It is too confronting not to tip.

We give him a euro, which is almost two Australian dollars, and pretty steep for a couple of strums of Zorba, but we don't want to be tight-fisted just yet, at the beginning of our trip.

The musicians move on and are instantly replaced by smiling African men squeezing through the tables and selling beads and wooden toys and tea towels, stuff no-one ever buys. One of them is a Denzel Washington look-alike with a fantastic body, and I let my dirty imagination loose for a minute. He could be in porn movies—or even ordinary movies—and make a fortune, but here he is trying to sell tea towels to disinterested tourists. It saddens me to think these happy handsome men are forced to do this kind of work (sell tea towels, not do porn); no-one ever buys anything from them, but they are on the streets with big smiles and bags of crap every night. Earlier we'd seen one enterprising African man playing a violin at the traffic lights, which you have to admit beats the hell out cleaning windscreens. But no-one gave him any money either. I like these African men—they are always cheerful and take rejection with a wide white-toothed smile—but I get thoroughly annoyed by the gipsy women standing at traffic lights looking bored and holding placards with badly spelled pleas for money for starving babies.

But never mind about hawkers and gipsies, this happy Athens scene is infectious. It puts us in a good mood, and we sit at our table far longer than the staff would like us to.

Every time it seems there might be a chance of a quiet moment among the clamour, the old grandpa gets off his chair and claps enthusiastically at the passers-by, singing in a croaky old voice. It never fails to attract a new bunch of people.

We leave this marvellous spot an hour later and walk through the crush to the end of the street, where we come across the bright but depressing golden arches of a fluorescently lit McDonald's. It breaks the spell like a bucket of icy water thrown over us, so we head quickly back to our hotel and make plans to visit the Acropolis in the morning—this time, in a neat and sober condition.

In 2003 the Acropolis does indeed look like the grand structure it once was. The restoration is almost complete, but there are many cranes and much scaffolding still sitting around on this hot June morning. There are also hundreds of tourists, paying 12 euros each to get in, buying maps, books, sunglasses, water and souvenirs.

Geoffrey still can't get over how silly the Greeks were not to realise all those years ago what a powerful tourist attraction and money-maker this icon is. He tends to rant on a bit about it.

'Look at how impressive it looks now,' he says and taps the columns the way carpenters do when they inspect a nice bit of woodwork.

And impressive it is, too. Seeing the formidable amount of scaffolding and machinery required to restore it now only makes you more awed to think how it was originally built without a single power tool more than 2500 years ago. All around us tour guides are giving their groups lectures on the history, but I don't think anyone ever takes it all in. It requires quiet thinking and much reading to comprehend the full scale of the history of monuments such as this.

In the mid fifth century BC, a man of vision, by the name of Pericles, persuaded the locals to begin an ambitious program of building in Athens. Work began on the Acropolis, with three contrasting temples and a monumental gateway. The Theatre of Dionysus, on the south slope, was built in the fourth century BC and the Theatre of Atticus Herodes was added in the second century BC.

The Theatre of Atticus Herodes makes the fine hair on my arms stand up—much the way the Grand Canyon did when I first saw it. This superb theatre was built by a wealthy Roman, Claudius Atticus Herodes, in memory of his wife Regilla. It was restored in 1955 and is used today for summer concerts. I yearn for the opportunity to sit in the floodlit amphitheatre on a hot night to watch a performance, but our time in Athens won't permit it, so I must satisfy myself by standing and staring down at the steep slope of the magnificent theatre for a long and thoughtful time. It is so absorbing that I don't even see or hear the hordes of tourists around me.

Later we wander around with the masses and make appropriate sounds of admiration at the iconic structure, and then we go into the Acropolis Museum to be further impressed. This is one of the most important museums in the world and houses many masterpieces of the ancient Greek civilisation, but we don't get much of a feel for it straight away because it is crowded and uncomfortable. Many of the works of art that were part of the Acropolis have been stolen, and it is the English bounder Lord Elgin who seems to have done the heftiest bit of pillaging (with the permission of the occupying Turks at that time). He sold his spoils, including the famous marble friezes, to the British government, and they are still not here in Greece, where they should be. The Greek authorities, who are at the moment building a new museum as part of the Olympic Games building project, want them back. Understandable, but the British government shows no sign of parting with them.

The collections now inside the museum include sculptures from the Archaic period, pediments of temples, plenty of magnificent Archaic horsemen, and parts of the Parthenon and the Erechtheum friezes, as well as many clay figurines and vases from the sanctuary of the nymphs.

We stand for long minutes staring at a sculpture of a man on a beautiful horse; only the lower part of the horseman's body remains, but it is still marvellous. He holds reins made of bronze in his left hand and wears sandals on his feet. It is a great composition, with flawlessly executed detail, one of the most beautiful equestrian statues ever created, and was made in the sixth century BC. We move on to admire a statue of a magnificent man with a six pack stomach and a huge barrel chest which seems to swell even though it is marble, and suddenly an official-looking woman marches through the crowds shouting 'Don touch plizz, don touch, move on.'

We hadn't even thought of touching. Why do these people always have such a bossy air about them, and make you feel like naughty children? And why am I frightened of them? Don't bother answering that—you're probably frightened of them too.

She then tells everyone to shut up. 'Quiet plizz, no talking plizz.'

No talking in a museum? We shut up obediently even though no-one else does, and shuffle out with the crowds, into the midday heat feeling miffed and a little disappointed at the museum experience. On our way down through the Plaka's streets we pass an old black-clad woman trying to sell an intricately hand-embroidered tablecloth to a man who is bargaining mercilessly with her.

'It is big, grand, big,' she says pleadingly as he offers her first 50 euros, then 40, then 30.

'It took me three months to do,' she entreats as he turns his back on her and then walks off.

This little scene makes me feel as anguished as the men fighting did the night before. Imagine slaving over something for three months and quite likely damaging your eyesight, and then having to stand on the street to try to sell it, pleading with cynical people to take it for a fraction of its value? Horrible.

We make our way through the roadworks, past the hoardings, around the scaffolding and through the general messy upheaval that is Athens this summer and decide it is not a good place to be at the moment.

Next year, when the Olympics are about to be staged, we are sure Athens will be a place of grandness again, but now it is just an awful mess. It is time to get on a ferry and sail off to a Greek island.

We had spent an impressive amount of time on the internet before we left, determined to know something in advance about the places we will visit. The ease of making inquiries, reservations and just generally finding out things on the internet still astounds me. With a tap of the mouse you can be in touch with someone thousands of kilometres away and he will talk back to you, almost always in a pleasing manner and almost always, instantly. Friendships form over simple hotel reservation arrangements, and before we leave Australia we are already on friendly terms with hotel owners (mostly called Nick or George) all over Greece.

You may think I am a silly old fool to get excited about something as commonplace as the World Wide Web, but if you once had to make all travel arrangements by slow mail or expensive telegram, you'd be pretty thrilled with instant communication too.

It seems ridiculous that I, a woman in her fifties (and looking pretty good for it, if I may say so, despite some sag in the mammary area) can remember a time when travel arrangements had to be made via formal letters that began with 'My Most Dear And Respectful Sir' and ended up with 'Obediently Your Humble Servant'. These ridiculous letters took weeks to arrive at their destination, and then you waited impatiently for several more weeks for a reply, looking out for the postman who let you know he was around via his whistle, and travelled his route on a bicycle.

The telephone was used only in the direst of emergencies, because an overseas call, something we called a trunk call, was a thing of monumental expense. If we did have the need, and the courage, to make a trunk call, we would have to go through an operator, and when we were finally connected we would shout at the person on the other end of the line as though he was a stone-deaf imbecile living in an open shed on Mars. We would always keep the call as brief (and so as cheap) as possible, leaving the person on the other end unsure about whether we wanted a hotel room or not.

Telegrams were used sometimes, but they usually meant someone had died, so we avoided them in order to not put the wind up the receiver. And it wasn't just travel arrangements that took forever to make. Imagine the snail's pace of work done in offices all over the country. Being an office girl from the age of fifteen, I started out on an old Underwood typewriter and grew into all this modern stuff, mostly with a great deal of reluctance. I can easily recall the delirium of excitement the girls in my office felt when the fax machine was introduced. We all gathered timidly around this astonishing item of terrifying technology for a serious lesson on how to send a fax. Really.

The most gratifying thing about the fax—far more satisfying than being able to send paperwork to someone across town and have them receive it within minutes instead of waiting for it to be delivered by a boy on a motor scooter—was that it made the telex operator redundant.

The telex itself was a huge and formidable machine the size of a car, always operated by a huge and formidable woman the size of a bus. With thunderous clacking noises it sent messages off to other formidable telex ladies who, no doubt, terrorised their own office girls at the other end. The telex operator was much like the lady in the Acropolis Museum: bossy as hell and so scary that even the chairman of the company was terrified of her. She would punch the keyboard on the telex machine with great force and glare at us at the same time as 5000 metres of tickertape stuff came out the end of her machine.

Anyway, the bossy telex operator is long gone from all our lives, and now we can chat on the Web to all the Nicks and Georges of Greece with the greatest of ease. We can look at pictures of their nice hotels, inquire about their families, vegetable plots, goats and sex life, and by the time we actually get over to their country and meet them face to face, we can be on such good terms that they immediately ask us about our own goats and our sex life. It's positively marvellous.

Planning a long overseas trip now, with all the fantastic visuals and information available on our computers in our homes, is almost as good as actually doing it—but nowhere near as riveting as reading about it right here.

SINGING NORWEGIANS ON A GREEK ISLE

Lesbos is the third biggest of the Greek islands, after Crete and Euboea. It belongs to the islands of the Eastern Aegean Sea and sits very close to Turkey. 'The flower of an eternal spring set on the blue waters of the Aegean, a vision that opens wide its modest beauty to the horizon, offering an invitation to love and promise.' This is what our guidebook says, and it's worth repeating here because a vision that opens wide its modest beauty is an agreeable image and a good way to start a chapter about this seductive island.

It is a fertile island with vast olive groves; it also produces wheat, wine and citrus fruit. Fishing and farming are significant industries, and tourism obviously brings in quite a few dollars each summer now. The island is big and prosperous enough to support an airport, which is convenient, because it's an overnight ferry trip from Athens otherwise. Its capital, Mytilene, is a place that has inspired artists since antiquity and is now home to 25 000 people. It has a wide picturesque harbour around which it is obvious that most of the town's life pulsates—banks, pastry shops, restaurants, florists and booksellers sit between large hotels, all overlooking the harbour. As soon as we arrive we head off to find the ancient theatre so signposted near the harbour, because if one is in Greece, one really should be looking for these sorts of things, not for females of the homosexual persuasion.

We can't find it, and give up after asking three people where it is and being told they didn't know. This doesn't make for a good start. Instead we go straight to the old Venetian castle overlooking the town, built in 1260, and wander around the crumbling walls, pretending to each other that this is culturally enlightening. No attempt appears to have been made at restoration. We are entirely alone here in the midday heat, and can't get inside the walls. While it might sound good to you—romping over castle ruins on a Greek island—it is actually boring, and it's way too hot and bothersome to be walking around on dry grass looking at crumbling old walls. We have time and castles aplenty to explore, and we feel the need to get in the hire car and get out of Mytilene because it is just a touch too city-like for us. We want the Greek countryside.

Lesbos was a centre of Bronze Age civilisation, a brilliant cultural centre from the seventh to sixth century BC, when the poets Alcaeus and Sappho were active here. Sappho is the one the gay women relate to, because she was gay herself and made lesbianism a trendy thing back then. She was born in the southern area of Skala Eressos, which is now the international mecca for lesbians and about to be a mecca for Ann and Geoffrey Rickard.

Lesbos is a blotch of a shape. That's the best way I can describe it. It has a long Italy-like leg running down the east side, and a huge bite in its middle where the Bay of Kalonis divides the east from the west. Its coastline stretches for 370 kilometres, and its population is about 100 000—it probably swells to a million during the busy summer season.

'Visit Vatera and Skala Eressos at the bottom of the island and Molyvos at the top of the island and you will think you have visited two very different Greek islands,' our friends on the Web had told us.

'The northern part of Lesbos is green and heavily treed, and the south is drier. Vatera and Skala Eressos in the south will remind you of Atlantic seaside communities without the commercialism.'

So down to the bottom of Lesbos, to Vatera and Skala Eressos, we shall head for many lazy days and wine-filled nights, and then we will go up to Molyvos for more of the same.

Skala Eressos is probably one of the few places in the world where homosexual women can relax and be themselves and meet like-minded women without having hordes of curious tourists staring at them— apart from when Geoffrey and I arrive. It is said to be a 'little pocket of Greece which is one of the most cosmopolitan areas of the island'.

Quite frankly, the thought of Skala Eressos excites us. But first we are going to Vatera, another place of great natural beauty, 50 kilometres from Mytilene, and with the longest beach on the island. Vatera is right at the bottom of the east side of the island, and has remained unaffected by the masses, which makes it most appealing to us. Tourists we may be ourselves, but we really do like places that lack other tourists. Vatera's beach has been rated as one of the best beaches in the Aegean: it is an impressive 10 kilometres long, and is protected from the summer northerly winds. This beach is apparently so good that it has been repeatedly awarded the Blue Flag of the EEC for its cleanliness and clear unpolluted waters.

Unfortunately, we dislike Vatera at first sight.

We can be shallow and judgemental people sometimes, we know, but Vatera has been recommended to us so glowingly that we expected to be veritably bowled over by its charms. And we are not.

We've had an exciting drive here from Mytilene, over winding hills and tall mountains. The road twisted dramatically around on itself, climbing and dipping, giving us an exhilarating roller-coaster ride. We've travelled over brown landscape and through green fields rich with olive trees and wild herbs. Actually, we have never seen so many olive trees in our lives. They are starkly striking and stoic things, growing out of hard, dry land, and the sight of so many of them is a reminder that this humble tree—and the even more unassuming olive itself—plays an important part in the universe.

As the road took us high in places we had picturesque views to small blue bays and clustered red-roofed villages. With our map spread over the dashboard we drove straight through the small villages of Vasilika, Polihnitos and Vrisa, eager to get to Vatera, too excited to stop and explore these sleepy little places.

Now that we are here, Vatera, with its long strip of gritty brown beach separated from boring brightly coloured hotels by a flat bitumen road, holds no appeal at all.

'There's nothing Greek about it,' I comment to Geoffrey. 'Where's the Greek whitewashed architecture, the cobbled streets filled with souvenir shops and cafés, the bougainvillea growing up walls, the donkeys, the fishing boats?'

This place is too new, too modern, too stark; a reminder of some of the uninteresting new developments in coastal towns in Australia.

Our hotel looks much like all the others lining the beachfront, but we have one of the rooms at the front—the others all sprawl back and face dry, undeveloped fields. We settle in, blaming each other as usual for making the decision to come to Vatera, and decide that the best thing we can do is go across the road to the hotel's small taverna—at least it's right on the beach—and eat.

The hotel owner's wife is an attractive, friendly lady who serves us an excellent pizza and a jug of wine. We immediately perk up and stop blaming each other.

It's late in the afternoon and the taverna is empty except for a large group of middle-aged people behind us, taking up two long tables. They look as though they are making their slow way through a long lunch. The beach is also quite empty; the sea is choppy and murky. It is nothing like my dream of clear calm waters in a picturesque cove.

Someone in the group behind us has a piano accordion, another a clarinet. They start playing mournful songs.

'This really is Greece, isn't it?' I ask Geoffrey as the group sing along to 'Harbour Lights' in cheerless voices. 'Harbour Lights' … you know that old Platters song? 'I saw the harbour lights, they only told me we were parting.' And we don't even have a harbour here!

The group sway together and seem to be on the verge of tears as the sad song fills the air in the small taverna. They clap morosely at the end and I feel like slitting my wrists.

But then things take a cheery turn as they launch into 'Hello Dolly', with a small amount of enthusiasm.

'Hello Dolly' on the clarinet on a Greek Island. Where are the bouzoukis, the tambourines, the Greek dancers? These are not English-speaking people but they know all the words to 'Hello Dolly' and 'Harbour Lights', and in its own strange way, this impromptu afternoon concert by the beach becomes quite fascinating.

'Smoke Gets In Your Eyes' comes next, and by this time I'm singing along with them. Our voices waft down the empty beach.

'Who are these people?' I ask our attractive hotel host the next time she makes her way past our table.

'They're Norwegians, all friends. They come every year for their holiday,' she says. 'They bring their own musicians with them. They love it here. They always have a singalong.'

There you go. Norwegians singing 'Smoke Gets In Your Eyes' on a Greek island every year. This is a lesson to all you travellers. Never expect the expected.

As they tunelessly embark on 'Nevertheless'—'Maybe I'm right, maybe I'm wrong, maybe I'm weak, maybe I'm strong, but nevertheless I'm in love with you'—they sound like a bunch of old drunks in their cups. It's only about five o'clock in the evening and blazingly sunny—there are hours to go before darkness and an appropriate time to get drunk and sing doleful songs. It's time to leave this melancholy scene … and melancholy is the right word, because as we walk off they swing into 'Come to me my melancholy baby'.

We take a stroll to try to cheer up but only feel more depressed as we pass garishly coloured hotels and new guesthouses, with evidence of many more being built. We retire to our hotel feeling disillusioned and unhappy.

In the morning the Norwegians are out in force at the breakfast smorgasbord, wearing shorts and brightly coloured T-shirts and plastic sun visors. They line up with trays for hard-boiled eggs, ham, thick bread, sweet cakes, cheese pastries and jam.

Europeans love sweet cakes for breakfast, which they're entitled to, of course, but it's something we can't get used to. We take coffee and bread and ham to a table as far away from the crowds as we can get in the spacious breakfast room, and look out across the road to the beach and decide we really have to open our minds and give Vatera a fair go.

Obviously the locals who have owned this land along the beachfront for generations recognise a good thing when it comes along—even if it is singing Norwegians—and they have begun to sell their land for development. Signs everywhere tell us that Vatera is fast becoming the Next Big Thing as far as holiday resorts go. We decide to spend the day exploring the beachfront and enjoying the beach, though the sea is still unpleasantly choppy and unappealing.

A family of six Norwegians crowds behind us in the breakfast room, despite the dozen empty tables spread around the room. They squeeze into the table and pull back chairs, knocking into me and making me spill my coffee. These Europeans are obviously so used to not having much space that they don't mind in the least crowding into yours. They sit on top of each other and smoke while others eat and don't seem to notice that this might be inconvenient for someone at all.

But I do envy them their capacity to enjoy absolutely anything. Despite their sad singing the night before, the Norwegians seem to be enjoying themselves immensely. Even eating something as simple as sweet cakes for breakfast seems to bring them much pleasure, and crowding over each other and banging chairs into foreigners is all part of the fun.

We finish our breakfast quickly and set off to explore the road running parallel to the beach. In between the new hotels are empty blocks of land and old stone houses that have escaped the developers' bulldozers—so far.

While it all lacks the atmosphere we expected in a Greek island beachside resort, we can now see why people would be attracted to Vatera. The hotels have all the conveniences tourists want, and the beach, just a few steps across the road, is lined with tavernas and shady trees. And with guaranteed hot dry weather in the summer, it's no wonder the Norwegians and people from northern Europe love it here.

We love the old shack-style buildings lying low and timid between the big hotels, which fortunately are not high-rise monsters—they're just three storeys high. Without exception, all the hotels have unbroken balconies running along their frontages. This is something I cannot get used to. Sitting on your hotel balcony just centimetres away from your neighbour is completely the opposite of what it is supposed to be, relaxing. I find it positively nerve-wracking. It takes away the anonymity of being in a hotel. Some may think that's a good thing; I don't.

When you are inside your room you are a stranger from your neighbour, unaware that anyone is even next door to you—unless, of course, they are particularly noisy—but the minute you take a step out onto this kind of balcony, you are forced into friendship. It is impossible not to nod and say hello to your neighbour when he is sitting less than a metre from you, separated by only a see-through bit of low balustrade. Minutes before, he was a stranger inside his own room, doing whatever things people do in the privacy of their hotel rooms—picking his nose or enjoying room service with his blow-up doll, for all I care—

but after that single step onto the balcony, you are forced into acknowledging each other, to make falsely cheerful conversation, until you step back inside your room and become strangers again, once more going about your dirty deeds. (In my case nothing more naughty than typing my travel notes so I can bring you whimsical asides such as this. Honestly.)

'Why don't the developers put screens up to separate each bit of balcony?' I ask Geoffrey as we wander along the beachfront gazing up to lines of people sitting side by side on their balconies.

'Why should they?' he says, because he doesn't get hung up on things like connecting balconies and doesn't mind sitting right on top of strangers on his bit of balcony.

We walk along, enjoying the empty blocks of land between the hotels, peering into the few old shacks left, stopping to count the number of healthy vegetables growing in small plots beside the old houses.

There are flourishing vegie patches everywhere, little oases of green among the dry brown grass and thistles. Pumpkins, tomatoes, potatoes, peppers, zucchini, onions and basil, all thrive. Our hotel hostess had told us proudly last night that all the vegetables in the hotel's dishes were from her garden, and that as many local products as possible were used in her hotel kitchen. We warm a little to Vatera.

We decide to spend the day on the beach, to allow our fondness to grow to love.

Unfortunately, all that grows is our annoyance with the place, and we retire to our hotel room later to think seriously about leaving.

That night we venture across the road again for dinner and eat delicious fried zucchini, a really good Greek salad and excellent steak. People at a nearby table are celebrating a family birthday; a young boy is the centre of attention. The family all dote on him and let him order anything he wants from the menu.

We enjoy eavesdropping on the family even though we can't understand a word they say. Out comes a big birthday cake and they all stand and sing a (Danish we think) version of 'Happy Birthday', ending with

'Raw raw raw'. Or should that be 'Roar roar roar'? Whatever. It sounds cute, and much better than 'Hip hip hooray'.

Just as we are beginning to enjoy the quiet evening, out come the Norwegians. They start singing those old songs again. I want to tell them I really could enjoy their singing if only they would get some more modern and lively stuff into their repertoire. Just as I am working up enough courage to do this, they strike up—I am not lying—an ear-splitting off-key version of 'God Save the Queen'. The English Queen! Not even their own! It is all deeply curious.

'What are they doing?' I ask our host again, the next time I catch her dashing past our table on her way to the Norwegians with huge trays of beer. 'They are rehearsing,' she says. 'One of them is having an important birthday on Thursday and they plan a really big night. This is just practice.'

This makes the decision for us. It is time to leave Vatera. We had planned to stay here for a couple of weeks, but the thought of lying on a gritty brown beach by choppy water all morning, wandering along a boring strip of road each afternoon, sitting on a balcony within centimetres of our neighbours each evening and listening to ridiculous English songs sung by Norwegians each night is just too gloomy. It is time to move on to Skala Eressos.

We want to immerse ourselves in a place with real Greek feeling. We want little laneways with crazy paving, shops selling silver jewellery, leathery old men playing with worry beads in cafés, Greek widows sorting olives, and brightly clad donkeys munching on grass … but above all else, we want lesbians.

PREHISTORIC BONES
IN VRISA

Although Skala Eressos could be just a short drive and then a quick ferry ride across the Bay of Kalonis from Vatera, there is no ferry, so a long drive halfway back up the island, following the bay all the way up, is required. It will take us a good day to make the drive if the roads are as windy as we are led to believe and we look forward to it. We'll stop and explore small villages this time and get more of a feel for the place.

The first stop comes just a few minutes up the road, at the tiny village of Vrisa. It's Sunday, and to say the village is sleepy this afternoon is quite an understatement. It is positively snoring. We drive into its narrow streets, empty now but for one other car behind us. We are looking for the Natural History Collection. We are filled with guilt at leaving Vatera so hastily and want to see a little of its history before we race off chasing lesbians.

Fortunately, the museum is open—nothing else is—and it's empty except for a good-looking director who takes one euro each off us and says he will give us a personal tour because obviously he has nothing else to do. Annoyingly, the car behind us has stopped too, and out come four middle-aged English tourists who join us. No-one else on the whole of Lesbos is interested in this museum at this time except us and these four other people, and we all have to arrive at the same time. It really pees me off, but that's because I can sometimes be a selfish bitch and like to have space to myself.

One of the English tourists is called Bill, and he's a big know-all. He wears shorts, knee-high socks and sandals, has a camera and a pair of binoculars around his neck, and an authoritative air about him.

Bill knows everything there is to know about every subject in existence—I'm sure you've met Bill yourself on your own travels—even the ancient history of Vatera and of the birds and creatures that roamed this place in prehistoric times, which we are going to hear all about from our director. But before he can speak, Bill does.

'That's a three-legged vulture buzzard,' he says as he enters the small bird room, pointing to a big stuffed bird behind a glass cabinet. I personally think it more closely resembles a white-breasted sea eagle, but I'm not about to say so.

The handsome director immediately corrects Bill and points out the bird's real name, which I've forgotten now, but Bill says yes he knew that already and was just testing the director's knowledge. Bill then goes on to name all the coiled snakes in the big jars lining the walls, and tells us all the length of their fangs and degree of their poison, and how many he has already seen alive or dead himself on the roads and fields during his two-week holiday on Lesbos. The polite director corrects him again, saying there is only one deadly snake on the island and it is rarely seen. This fazes Bill not in the least.

We spend half an hour in the small museum, looking at displays of two-million-year-old fossils and the ancient bones of prehistoric animals and stuffed birds and snakes in jars, all indigenous to the area (which the white-breasted sea eagle isn't, as you clever readers would know), and although I find it interesting at first, like all these things, once I get my head around the mind-boggling number of years that man and beast can be traced back in Greece, it becomes boring. Looking at bones and rocks can only hold my interest for a certain amount of time; Bill with the binoculars, on the other hand, could examine them endlessly.

While the director is in deep lecture mode, pointing out maps showing prehistoric landmasses and volcanic changes, with Bill listening rapturously and everyone else bored to distraction, Geoffrey takes a step back and bumps into a glass cabinet, sending dozens of two-million-year-old bones flying off its shelves and banging all around the cabinet.

Everyone is horrified by the noise and mess except Bill, who looks deeply annoyed at the interruption. The director undoes the cabinet and rearranges the bones. He is the epitome of civility and says it is no problem, even though Geoffrey has probably shattered some of the ancient bones and Bill looks as though he wants to shatter Geoffrey's own ancient bones.

Finally we compose ourselves, and the director points out some fossil bits from a giant prehistoric turtle.

'There is a replica of the creature out in the back garden, made from a mould of a Volkswagen car. It is the exact size,' he says.

This excites Bill tremendously, as it does us, and the six of us rush eagerly outside to see the giant turtle that Bill insists on calling a tortoise. It sits in the middle of the garden in an enormous glass cabinet, and I must say, it is bloody marvellous. We all gather around the glass structure, oohing, aahing, and try to take photos through the glass, which is almost impossible because of reflections and sunlight and all that stuff.

Geoffrey presses his camera to the glass and Bill immediately rushes over with advice about lenses, angles, zooms and other photographic jargon that is all meaningless to Geoffrey, who can only just manage to push the on button on his new digital camera. We do manage a few photos though—and they come out all right actually, much to our surprise.

Later, when looking through our guidebook, we find that Bill is indeed correct, and this thing is a tortoise and not a turtle, damn it. It used to roam around Vatera a couple of million years ago, no doubt doing whatever it felt like, because it was 2.5 metres long, 1.6 metres high and weighed 1000 kilograms. A Volkswagen car was actually used to make the model we were looking at. A cast for the tortoise shell was made from the body of the car, with enormous front legs installed where the front tyres were and the back legs where the back wheels would be, if you can imagine that. It really is very good, and should you ever find yourself in Vatera, please visit the Natural History Collection—and just pray Bill with the binoculars has long since departed.

We stroll into the tiny church in the small square opposite the museum and check it out for a full five minutes. I love to think about the people who come here to worship: what they are like, how they live, how important it is for them to have a place to pray. The Greek Orthodox Church is a powerful force in Greece, and we are led to believe that most Greeks visit their church regularly. This church has an impressive bright gold chandelier, at least 2 metres wide, hanging from the ceiling. There are frescoes and candles and rich trappings everywhere, even though it is a tiny church in a small village. But five minutes in here is enough.

We continue our drive to Skala Eressos, determined to take our time, make plenty of stops and see the thermal baths, the Petrified Forest, and the many little coves and beaches along the way. Of course we do none of that. The Petrified Forest is 60 kilometres out of our way and we really can't be bothered with the thermal baths right now. We know they are all over the island and that we will have plenty of time to thermally infuse ourselves later. We drive through a stark landscape of vast hills and deep valleys, up and down winding roads with hairpin bends—and everywhere there are those silver-grey olive trees.

We do stop at the tiny fishing village of Skala Polihnitos, right on the sea, and wander around for ten minutes looking at the fishing boats, the teeny supermarket where a couple of kids are buying a huge bag of potatoes and a six-pack of beer—for their parents, we hope. That's it, we say, and on we go.

'Lesbos must support the entire Greek olive industry,' I remark to Geoffrey as we drive through yet more olive groves. Unbeknown to me, he has already read the guidebook. 'The eleven million or so olive trees on Lesbos are reputed to be the most productive oil-bearing trees in the Greek islands,' he says. 'Crete produces more and better quality oil, but no other island is so dominated by the olive monoculture.'

I'm impressed.

The olive trees are lovely in the breeze. They shimmer and show both the silver and green sides of their leaves, and with so many clumped together they make for a mass of wavering, shimmering landscape.

The day is brilliantly sunny with a vast blue sky, and the heat comes in relentlessly through the windscreen, fighting with the air conditioning. We drive through Lisvori, Vasilika and Athaderi, all small and interesting villages with tightly clustered houses and narrow streets. Some of the streets are so skinny that the car almost scrapes the sides of buildings. We are grateful that it is Sunday and there is almost no traffic around, because if we met someone coming the other way in one of these villages, one of us would have to back up many kilometres of tight winding road. In one village we get hopelessly lost in the labyrinth of narrow streets and pass by the same tiny taverna a dozen times. An old bloke sitting alone outside among the empty tables and chairs stares at us and fiddles with his worry beads each time we pass. As we drive by him for the sixth time I offer a wave, feeling we know him by now. On the seventh trip he waves back.

Around and around the tight corners we go, sweating and stressing —it is very tight, and we feel we could quite possibly get stuck in a claustrophobic alleyway and have to stay here for the rest of our lives. The doors of the houses open right out on to the street and the feeling that we are in a pedestrian area is strong.

None of these villages has shown any sign of modern life. The dwellings are so old and rustic that it is like stepping back in time.

Nothing looks as if it has changed in hundreds of years. It could be quite exciting if only we could relax and enjoy it, but the stress of being lost overrides everything else. Nasty words fill the inside of the car.

On one especially narrow part we come across a red car in front of us, driving slowly but confidently through the tight streets and making its careful way around the sharp corners. We follow it, sure that it will lead us out of the village and back to the main road. Where it actually leads us is down a long steep road and to the end of a driveway that happens to be the driver's home. The driver, yet another leathery old man, stops, gets out, looks at us with a bemused expression and shrugs his shoulders as if to say, 'You complete morons, don't you know you'll never get yourselves out of this tight spot now?' but then obviously takes pity on us. He stays to help us manoeuvre our way out. I get out too and watch Geoffrey reverse a few millimetres, then go forward a couple of millimetres, and repeat this process several thousand times with the old man shouting encouragement.

'Ela, ela, ela,' he says over and over, which we think this is a multi-purpose Greek word for 'come, go, back, forward, here, there, shut up, what-big-stupid-yobbos-you-are'.

Our car is not automatic and Geoffrey has long ago forgotten how to use gears smoothly, so there is much revving and gear crunching and cursing, and more cries of 'ela, ela, ela' from the old man (and me, by now), and after fifteen tortuous minutes Geoffrey finally manages to get the car facing the right way. I leap in and we rev and curse and drive up the steep hill, me blowing kisses to the old man because I am so grateful for his help. We would never have got out without him. I do find Greeks very helpful, especially the splendidly weathered old blokes. If you stop to ask directions of one old man, within a minute ten others have joined him, all shouting and gesticulating and jabbing fingers at your map. Sometimes scuffles have almost broken out when one man disagrees with the advice of another. I am guessing this, though, because it is all Greek to me.

From the twisting road that follows the bay around its length we have views to imposing mountains on one side and sparkling small inlets on the other. All the bays have the word 'Skala' in front of them, which I took to mean 'beachside' until I looked it up and found it meant 'harbour'. Much the same. It's all gorgeous.

We drive on through the day, and slowly make our way around the huge bay to take a detour off the main road to Apothikes, a particularly tiny bay we have seen from the top of the road and have to visit because it looks so enticing.

It requires a three-kilometre drive along an unmade road, which jars my boobs so badly I have to hang onto them. Tall volcanic rock formations line the road and look so perfect they could be abstract sculptures created by some of Greece's contemporary sculptors.

The moon-like landscape reminds me strongly of Sunshine in Melbourne, where I spent most of my formative years, and a place where many Greek immigrants settled in the 1950s and 1960s. The countryside here could explain why the Greek people seemed to assimilate and settle in so easily in Sunshine—it is landscape they were familiar with. My childhood was spent playing in this environment and watching old Greek ladies dressed in head-to-toe black, bending over the side of the road picking thistles, I assume to cook and eat.

New houses have been built in this tiny place right on the bay. They are in the same stone and architectural style as the older ones, but painted blue, pink and pale yellow. They have thriving trees and lush grapevines in their gardens that contrast ridiculously with the thistles in the older homes.

It is hot and still; there is no wind, not even a light breeze. We sit down under the trees at the only tiny taverna in the place. To me this is as close to Greek heaven as I can get. An unpretentious taverna, mamma cooking, papa playing cards nearby, an invitation to go into the kitchen to choose your meal, the daughter waiting tables, boats bobbing on the water, fishing nets jumbled on the stone-walled jetty, scruffy cats prowling beneath the tables, kids throwing pebbles in the water, Greeks all around us, a grandpa sitting at one of the tables in his best Sunday shirt and pants, with grandma fussing over the kids. I love it.

We order a Greek salad, some small fried fish, a glass of wine and a Mythos beer. While we wait, I slip out of my skirt and into the water (I did have my swimsuit on underneath—don't worry, I would never upset the locals). The water is deep, beautifully cool on my hot, dry skin and so clear I can see the rocks two metres below me. I look down to my red painted toenails, so clear in the clean water, as tiny fish swarm beneath me. I come back and sit on the wicker chair, dripping through the weaving, and dry in the heat before our meal has even arrived.

We eat the small fried fish and the best Greek salad we have had to date—sweet red tomatoes, delicious creamy fetta, red onion, black olives, fruity olive oil. We give the small fish heads to an appreciative cat that gobbles them and bobs his head up for more. One of the Greek families packs up to leave, and mamma, papa, three kids, an uncle and an aunt (or friends) all climb into a small wooden boat.

Geoffrey dips the bread into the oil at the bottom of his salad bowl and declares his happiness.

There is no hotel, no jewellery shop, no sign of modern tourist life—nothing at all except the taverna. It is as unpretentious as you could want, and our bill for this memorable experience comes to a mere eight euros, which the delightful girl who has served us mistakenly says is 'eight hundred euros'—she's practising her English—and then goes into fits of embarrassed laughter at her mistake. This is the Greek experience we so wanted. Not a Norwegian on the end of a clarinet in sight.

On we drive, through yet more dramatic countryside. I read from the guidebook to Geoffrey, to excite him further about Skala Eressos.

'The cosmopolitan life in summer attracts many tourists who come to enjoy the sun and the sea as well as the hospitality of Lesbos, presented in the best possible way. Furthermore, large numbers of homosexual women from throughout the world, women who idolise the ancient poetess Sappho, regularly gather at Skala Eressos every summer, giving the area a global flavour. This is a district that still boasts a few of its ancient glories: ancient Eressou with its stadium, theatre, agora, prytaneum, and the temples of Dionysus, Poseidon, Apollo and Athena, with the harbour and settlement which has spread back from the beach up to the site of Xokastro on the slopes of the hill where most of the finds were discovered.

'South of Vigla are the remnants of a Roman reservoir, and next to it the ruins of two towers, one Venetian and the other Turkish. There are even the ruins of the early Christian basilicas of Atentelis, with its lovely mosaics, and Agios Andreas, situated next to another two churches of the same name.'

'So how about all that?' I ask Geoffrey as I put the book down.

'Yeah, sounds really good. Read the bit about the homosexual women again,' he says as we finally pull into the outskirts of Skala Eressos.

BEAUTIFUL LADIES

It is love at first glimpse between the Rickards and Skala Eressos. The streets of the town that border the beach are closed to cars, so we leave our car in the dusty car park and wander past small shops selling books, jewellery, souvenirs and beach paraphernalia. It is energetic and exciting, and when we get down to the sea and look along a seemingly never-ending line of attractive cafés and bars, all with bamboo-covered decks jutting right out over the sand to the clear calm water, we don't think we could want for more. And there they are right before us—wall-to-wall lesbians.

They are all shapes, sizes, nationalities and ages, and they certainly look intent of having a good time. It's fantastic.

We have inquired with a friendly young man in a crammed souvenir shop about accommodation and he has told us to come back in half an hour: he has something perfect for us for 25 euros a night. This pleases us immensely. Twenty-five euros is less than 50 Australian dollars. I had the impression he was going home to remove his old mother from her accommodation and give it to us, but Geoffrey thinks he is waiting for his partner to come back to mind the shop while he shows us the place. We don't much care what he does, because by now we are sitting in a café right on the beach sipping mineral water and eavesdropping on lesbians. (Please don't tut-tut. You would too.)

Right behind us is a table of four English women talking excitedly. The leader of the conversation is a huge lady with a short back and sides haircut and a tattoo of a dragon on her fleshy upper arm. She wears a pale blue singlet and big khaki shorts, and her breasts are so operatic in size that they spill out of the sides of her singlet and flow impressively down to the table.

She is a person you would not argue with on a dark night. She is what I found out later from my beautiful lesbian hairdresser back home in Australia, a dyke. Ghastly word, I know, but one my hairdresser uses quite freely because she herself is a lipstick lesbian. There is a big difference, apparently, and it pays for lesbian greenhorns like us to find these things out if we plan to be in the company of these women, which we do, because we like them very much. A lipstick lesbian is one who loves dressing up in feminine froth and wearing lots of make-up. The other sort is the short back and sides, make-up free, singlet-wearing type.

Our lesbian friend behind us obviously falls into the latter category. (Oh, really?) I have my back to her now and can't see her, but Geoffrey can, and he is seething with curiosity. She talks fast and non-stop about subjects as varied as cooking, her preference in women, and the size of her bosom. And the funny thing is, her voice is completely at odds with her size: it's high-pitched, sweet and lovely—like a tiny angel talking.

'I love to cook my fish with white wine and parsley wrapped in a bit of foil in the oven,' she says in her mellifluous voice to her three mates, immediately followed by, 'I find as I get older, my preference for women is those aged over fifty, and one day I really would love to be able to run on the beach without getting a black eye from my swinging bosom. I saw a photo in a medical book recently of a man with testicles so huge they came down to his knees. I always put garlic in with the white wine on my fish. It's bad enough getting a black eye from your boobs when you run, but having enormous testicles must be like having a big pair of tits swaying between your legs when you walk. Shall we have another beer?'

I am not exaggerating.

Geoffrey is enthralled.

One of the other lesbians in the group is celebrating the first anniversary of her coming out, and she's receiving hearty congratulations from the others, as well as small admonishments for not doing so sooner, because she is not a young woman and has suffered unnecessarily with her secret for too many uncomfortable years. At another table a lone middle-aged lesbian sits in her swimsuit reading a book and sipping a juice. Another single approaches her.

'Are you enjoying it?' she asks.

'My book or my orange juice?' the first lesbian answers flirtily, and our heads swing away from the conversation behind us in the hope that we might be witnessing a chat-up in front of us. Geoffrey, being a typical man, is wriggling with excitement.

'She's on the prowl,' he whispers. This is a coarse expression—and he is not a coarse man—but by now we are both caught up in the whole lesbian pick-up scene. Then the reader's girlfriend comes out of the water—short hair, big shoulders, snorkel in hand—and walks proprietorially over to the couple. The prowler retreats.

We stay as long as we can, shamelessly eavesdropping and loving every minute of it, and then head back to find our man with the accommodation.

He has a studio apartment for us, in his mother's modern and attractive apartment complex, just 100 metres from the beach. It is not a very big room, but it has a tiny kitchenette and is more than adequate for 25 euros a night.

We settle in and Geoffrey unpacks our bulging suitcases, putting everything away in wardrobes and drawers—we intend to stay in this place a long time, and it will be marvellous not to live out of a suit-case. I never pack or unpack myself since the time Geoffrey accused me of packing too much air. That man can fit another half a suitcase of clothes into a suitcase already overflowing. He cannot tolerate wasted space, and when I thoughtlessly packed my walking shoes with-out stuffing them first with pants, bras and socks he almost had a small breakdown (and yes, he really can fit all those things inside a pair of my big walking shoes). Now I just sit on the bed and watch him pack and unpack, issuing helpful instructions—'Mind my gin bottle', 'Make sure the lid is properly on my moisturiser', 'I'll need those shorts, so keep them near the top' … that sort of supportive stuff. If I had known how good it was having someone pack and unpack for you I would have packed more air long ago. Now, when I'm in need of something, I just say, 'A bra would be nice' and Geoffrey burrows into the case and finds it in a shoe. 'And a pair of clean undies would go nicely with it,' I add, and off he tunnels into the case again, coming up with a pair he has packed inside a T-shirt inside a pair of shorts inside a handbag. He really is that good.

We sit on the tiny patio outside our studio, near an ornamental foun-tain, but we are right near the complex's gate and lesbians keep com-ing in and leaving the gate open which annoys us, and then a swarm of mosquitoes invade the fountain area and that annoys us more.

We are not comfortable, but Geoffrey has spied a heavily laden apri-cot tree just outside the gate, along the dusty road leading to the beach, so he likes it right here. He does not want to change. He gathers a handful of apricots and we have a little feast with our gin and warm tonic. Then the mosquitoes get the better of us so we go out looking for dinner.

The beach has settled down in the early evening: the water is calm, the sky is mauve, and a lone lesbian walking along the water's edge is beautifully silhouetted. The rocks rising from the sea and the moun-tains beyond are illuminated pale lavender and it is more than we hoped Skala Eressos would be.

We choose the first taverna we come to on the beach and order a plate of dips, a bean dish, squid, stuffed eggplant, and a half litre of house wine.

'Will that be enough food, do you think?' we ask our waiter.

'Yes, I think so,' he replies and then brings out giant platters of food, enough to feed all the lesbians on Lesbos.

'What have we done?' I ask Geoffrey, but he's too busy scooping his bright pink caviar dip onto a chunk of bread. The food is good, though the presentation is awful. Presentation is a concept not known to most Greek chefs; they just plonk, throw or splatter the food onto the most basic of plates and send it out of the kitchen. But food presentation in this marvellous setting is a thing of no importance, so I'll shut up. It is a hearty meal and we enjoy it so much we greedily call for another half litre of wine and then can't face even a glass of it. We waddle out and take a walk along the beachfront to check out the other places.

Lesbian paradise is all I can say. We are one of only a handful of heterosexual couples here, but no-one is about to stare, or even give us a glance. We think it is terrific for like-minded women to have a place of their own where they can holiday and hang out and be comfortable, apart from when idiots like us come and gawk at them. Actually, I am being unkind to us. We haven't really gawked, just listened in to conversations, and we have done that discreetly, apart from the time Geoffrey craned his neck at an alarming angle towards the table behind us. Skala Eressos might be known internationally to gay women as their own Greek island getaway, but it is also a beautiful holiday place for families and 'mature' people like us. It has all the beach activity and fabulous sea you could ask for, surrounding hills and pretty villages nearby, and, we discover later, a delightful outdoor cinema—and of course plenty of ruins and history should we feel the urge to go forth and explore.

Tonight the whole beachfront is alive and bustling. Music comes from funky bars and cafés, shops are brightly lit and doing a brisk trade, waiters are running back and forth from kitchens to tables with dishes of moussaka and Greek salads.

We retire to bed full of food and contentment, only to endure a night of torture. The air-conditioning doesn't work and we are forced to open the windows, whereupon swarms of pesky mosquitoes come in and we toss and turn so much Geoffrey gets up and goes out to walk in the dark night.

I try to doze, but it is impossible.

In the morning we ask to move to another apartment where the air-conditioning works. As the complex is fairly empty it isn't a problem, apart from packing up all our gear again … well, Geoffrey packing it. He says he spent the night wandering the beach, too scared to sit on a bench in case he looked like an old tramp and got beaten up. As the population of Skala Eressos is 99.9 per cent women I thought it a bit girlie of him. But I didn't say so.

Our new studio is much more comfortable, and mosquito free. We can prepare a modest lunch in the small kitchenette, which saves us eating out every day—not that the tavernas are expensive, but everything in Greece is cooked in vats of olive oil. Even the vegetables are soaked in the stuff. Fixing ourselves a sandwich of dry bread and tomatoes is only a small way to combat the calorie intake, but it helps.

The only downside of the studio is the bathroom, which is tiny, windowless and dark—it is like going into a small, dark, torture chamber. Europeans don't do bathrooms very well. It's a space thing, we know. We are used to bathrooms the size of the average European lounge room. We have adjusted to cramped showers, and put up with elbows knocking into walls as we clean our teeth, but we cannot adjust to this Greek thing of not putting toilet paper down the loo. Everywhere we go there are signs in bathrooms warning against this habit. The Greek sewerage pipes are so ancient they cannot cope with toilet paper.

'Use the bin provided' we are told by a sign with a forbidding red cross slashed across a hand recklessly throwing paper down the loo. I remember thirty-odd years ago in Greece on our motorbike trip using a public toilet with such a sign. There was an open mesh wastepaper receptacle on the back of the door for used toilet paper, about nose level as you sat down. It was full to overflowing, and the sight still comes calling on me in my nightmares all these years later. So now I absolutely refuse to put my toilet paper anywhere other than down the toilet, and if I am responsible for stuffing up the entire sewerage system on lovely Lesbos I apologise most profoundly, here and now, to the Minister for Sewerage. Really, I am sincerely sorry about that.

I don't know how the antiquated sewage system in Greece is going to cope during the Olympics. I doubt foreigners will heed warnings about only putting used toilet paper in a wastepaper bin. Imagine the impact of a couple of extra million people in the country all putting their paper down the toilet at once.

I don't wish to get into horror toilet stories, but all travellers have at least one, don't they? Entire websites are devoted to travellers' toilet tales, and they make for ghastly but fascinating reading. One story that stands out came from a bloke who went to a trendy and expensive seafood restaurant in Asia. The restaurant sat in the middle of a man-made island complete with a fish-filled moat from which you chose your fish for dinner. The waiters scooped your chosen fish out with a net and took it away and cooked it—and fish couldn't be any fresher than that. After the entrée course, this bloke went to the toilet to do what he had to do (okay, number two), and realised that the toilet was no more than a hole in the floor and that his business fell into—yes—the moat below, to swim along merrily with the fish. Needless to say, he didn't stay for the main course.

I'll say no more on that subject.

Geoffrey gathers apricots from the tree each morning for our breakfast and we have them with our coffee and bread, and feel virtuous at such a Spartan beginning to each day. We fall into a lazy, sunny, holiday routine. I take long afternoon walks by myself along the beach and then up to the villages behind the seafront, passing farm-houses and fields of bright green stuff that I think is fodder for cows or donkeys. I am not a rural woman so I am not sure what it really is, but it has a strong peppery smell and looks lush and green against the dry brown of the rest of the landscape. I discover a sprawling resort at the end of the beach, past the farmhouses, sitting large and lonely among undeveloped dry fields. It looks immense and soul-less, with clusters of yellow, blue and pale green buildings surrounding an Olympic-size pool and a neat garden area. Hundreds of deckchairs around the pool support bulky oiled bodies. I hate it on sight. But I'm curious enough to go in for a further look, walking down a long driveway flanked by oleander bushes. The grounds are immaculately manicured, but it all looks ridiculous right next door to brown fields of thistles. It makes me shudder and rush back to the charm of our boutique studio complex. Geoffrey has risen from his afternoon siesta and been for a stroll. He has noticed a sign on a telegraph pole announcing a party tonight.

'Come along and meet new friends,' it says. 'It starts at midnight. Bring your own food and drink.' It matters not that all of the new potential friends will be lesbians; I want to go.

'We can't go, it's not right,' Geoffrey says.

'But everyone is obviously invited and lesbians are not allowed to discriminate,' I tell him, but he doesn't look convinced. I am doing this only in your interests, dear reader. It is my duty to venture into the unknown to bring you as many colourful travel tales as I can. I'd much prefer just to have an early night.

I spend hours swimming in the clean water. Every swim is a highlight. But no matter how hard I try to relax in the water I simply cannot feel safe in the ocean. Like all Australians, I have a deep respect for the ocean. When there are weekly news reports of yet another poor soul being drowned or having a leg bitten off by a shark, you tend to be cautious on our beaches. I rarely go out further than knee deep in Australia and never ever go out of my depth. Yet here in Greece, where there seem to be no treacherous rips or strong undercurrents, or indeed, even woman-eating sharks, I cannot get over the thought that a frolic in deep water could well see me carried out to sea to end up in Athens. While everyone else here swims way out towards the horizon and floats and paddles blissfully for hours, I keep casting anxious looks back to shore to make sure it is within easy reach. On one of my glances back today I spy an octopus hanging on a piece of string over one of the tavernas, drying in the sun. It is a scene so quintessentially Greek that I swim in and take twenty photos of it. As it turns out, we find these freshly caught octopus hanging out to dry in tavernas all over Greece and take a hundred photos of them (really, we do), but seeing it for the first time still remains a thrilling memory.

Tonight we order the chargrilled octopus, served simply with lemon wedges, and find it hard and chewy; we agree to content ourselves with just looking at them and photographing them. We then eat egg and potato salad, stuffed vine leaves and a mini pizza, and once again feel disgustingly full and cannot see how we can possibly stay up until midnight for the lesbian party. We wander along the beachfront to try to walk the food off and to wake ourselves up, but it's impossible. 'I think we are going to have to forget the party,' Geoffrey says, and I reluctantly agree. Sorry about that. I did so want to bring you details of sexy female orgies where we were being gently coerced to join in and Geoffrey was last seen being buried alive in scented womanly flesh, but alas, it is not to be. You'll just have to try to visualise it. We wander past the outdoor cinema and take a peek in. *Lord of the Rings* is playing and we are tempted to pull up a couple of the plastic chairs—if we did we'd be the only people there, apart from the projectionist—but tiredness has overcome us and we head back to our studio.

In the morning we go for a long walk up to the outskirts of the village and spend the morning poking around the fields, trying to convince ourselves that we are exercising. We head back towards the beach and check out the big resort building again, because Geoffrey has not yet seen it. We wander right inside and around the pool area this time, looking at all the well-fed oiled bodies lounging on deckchairs, reading, sunning, sleeping. Some are doing archery and many are sitting in a café by the pool eating American-style hamburgers and French fries. It is so outrageously un-Greek it almost brings us to tears.

We walk on and on down the back roads until we come to a remote part of the beach, far from the resort section. We decide to walk the length of the beach back, and within minutes realise our mistake. This is the nude beach, and there, standing out spectacularly among the abundant flesh of a thousand lesbians, is our friend with the gorgeous voice, naked as the day she was born and weighing at least 100 kilograms more than she did on that day. She is sitting up, her giant breasts and stomach flowing down to the sand like molten lava. She is holding court again, and has a group of avid listeners.

We keep our eyes away but her melodious voice carries clearly to us.

'I just can't stay in a relationship with a younger woman now that I have turned forty, and I always grill my chicken on the barbecue rather than roast it, so much more flavour, and my last girlfriend just couldn't relate to a more mature mind.'

And so it goes.

We walk on with our eyes averted, but it doesn't prevent us catching awful glimpses of areas and orifices that are best kept hidden. Try as you can not to look, it is impossible, especially when nudists insist on getting up and dashing about. I have nothing at all against nudity—good on people who want to get an all-over tan. It's just that I don't think anyone over the age of twenty-five looks good without clothes. And why don't nudists just lie on the beach quietly instead of going all sporty? Why do they insist on playing beach cricket and volleyball, and sometimes even having leapfrog races? It's the same all over the world. I have never been on a beach where the nude people were happy to sit reading a book, with just the occasional quick dash into the water. They always, always, insist on leaping, running, jumping and frolicking.

Which is what they are doing right now, and we can't get out of here fast enough.

'I think that big lesbian who loves her chicken with garlic and women over fifty is going to haunt us for the rest of our stay on Lesbos,' I tell Geoffrey, and he heartily agrees.

I am sure you have had that experience too. When you go somewhere foreign and you see someone on the plane or train on the way there, and then keep bumping into them everywhere for the next two weeks? You never actually speak, but there is an instant hit of recognition as you sit next to them in a café, or run into them at the bakery, or see them at dinner. By the end of two weeks you are almost, but not quite, on speaking terms. We have a feeling our big lesbian chatterbox will be with us for the length of our stay.

And of course this proves to be true.

At three in the morning the roar of a motorbike, the crashing of gates and banging of doors outside our studio wakes us. A whole colony of lesbians has returned to the apartment next door after a party, and they are not finished celebrating yet. They sit right outside our window, drinking, and singing, talking and yes—you guessed it—there she is, voice as sweet as ever.

'I have known I was a lesbian since I was three,' she says. 'Do you know how to make the most melting lamb shanks on earth? Cook them for three hours in the oven, it always works. Wasn't that a fantastic party? Did you see that babe with the luscious lips? Always seal your lamb shanks in oil before you put them in the oven though, and then splash a bit of red wine over them.'

You don't believe me, do you?

PETRIFIED FORESTS AND QUAINT HARBOURS

Our weeks at Skala Eressos go by in a blur of beach lazing, swimming, eating, drinking and lesbian-watching. We haven't left this seaside resort at all apart from our walks into the small villages. We haven't sought any culturally enlightening museums or interesting ruins. But we have rested and relaxed, and now we feel we have intruded on the space of these interesting women enough. Not that we have gate-crashed their soirées or even dared to speak to anyone on the beach or in the cafés. It's just that this is so wholly their place that we want to leave it to them. We are thrilled to have shared it with them for this unforgettable time, and feel we are now full card-carrying honorary lesbians ... especially Geoffrey.

We spend our last day on the beach, hiring deckchairs and umbrellas for a reasonable six euros each, and sit in comfort, slapping sun lotion on every bit of exposed skin because it is very hot and there is no respite from the sun apart from the little bit of shade beneath our umbrellas.

By now we are thoroughly used to being with women who love women, and don't even blink when the attractive couple next to us hold hands, kiss, or gently stroke suntan lotion onto each other. Almost everyone on the beach is female, and almost all are topless. Geoffrey sits hairy and masculine among the feminine flesh and feels perfectly comfortable.

Nearly all the women have delicate pale pink areolas, a tell-tale sign that they have never been pregnant or given birth. For those of you who don't know (and if you're a bloke it's quite possible you really don't), a woman's areola—that round bit around the nipple—turns copper brown when she becomes pregnant, and it never changes back to that virgin pink colour again. I was twenty-nine when I had my first pregnancy, and the browning areola thing came as a bit of a shock, I can tell you. I was so ignorant I didn't even know what a uterus was, and yes I know that's hard to believe, but we didn't have those sealed sections in *Cleo* back then giving us advice on body changes during pregnancy and handy tips on masturbation techniques. I only found out about the areola change when I was in hospital, about to give birth for the second time, and the doctor brought around a bunch of medical students to examine me.

'This woman has obviously already had a pregnancy; she has secondary areola,' he said, pointing at my big fat breasts with their big fat brown circles.

Secondary areola. I never knew such a thing existed. It sounded like something you'd order at a trendy bistro. 'Can I have a side dish of secondary areola with my house-cut chips please.'

For months after that I went around saying 'secondary areola' out loud—with both words having four syllables, they had a nice sound when you put them together. (You have to say 'secondary areola' out loud to appreciate the lovely sound it has … go on, try it.) After I'd bored everyone to distraction about areolas, I promptly forgot all about them and have never given them a thought again until now, now that a never-ending pale pink field of them surrounds me. Anyway, enough about the changing colours of areolas.

We spend our last day in a lazy haze on the beach. A couple in front of us gives us a fifteen-minute erotic show when one of them, a tall slim woman, begins stroking lotion onto the other. She has elegant slim hands and she gently pats the oil on with such sensuous movements that everyone close by stares, riveted. First she does her partner's fleshy stomach and plump breasts with light feathery strokes, then she pulls one of the shapely legs right up and over her own body and applies the lotion from the middle of the thigh right down to the tips of the toes, giving each toe loving attention, then stroking the feet soothingly before sweeping up the calves to the thighs again, going dangerously close to the crotch area. It is so erotic I want to be a lesbian, for all of five minutes.

Geoffrey looks all flustered and then volunteers to go up to our studio and bring back drinks. Minutes later he comes down with a bottle of gin and little bottles of tonic—and ice, all wrapped in bags within bags. He makes drinks up for us right there on the sand and we tinkle the ice in our glasses, making all the lesbians jealous.

'Sorry, I forgot the lemon,' Geoffrey says as we sip.

'I forgive you,' I say generously.

We have our last dinner at one of the beachfront tavernas, sitting beneath strings of freshly caught octopus, and then take a long walk on the beach to say goodbye to this delightful place before heading back to our studio and falling into a deep sleep. I should have guessed we would not be leaving Skala Eressos without one last encounter with our favourite lady, and sure enough, she doesn't disappoint. Just before dawn, her honeyed voice wakes us from a deep sleep. It seems she has friends staying in the studio apartment next-door to ours, and she's out there again, drinking and talking into the dawn.

'Vegetables are easier to cook in the microwave than the steamer, and I've never had so much sex in my life as I have since I arrived here.'

It all comes wafting in our window cheering us until daylight, when she gives her friends a recipe for steak and kidney pudding, several loud kisses and takes her leave on her motorbike.

We will miss her terribly.

Our drive from Skala Eressos to the top of the island to Molyvos—our next stop for a long languorous spell—takes us past the Petrified Forest. This is a place we have wanted to see very much, because it looks eerily fascinating. The Petrified Forest is set in a deep dry brown valley and is only one of two in the world: the other is in Arizona, and is not nearly so impressive, apparently.

We are the only people here, and after five minutes down in the immense dry valley we can see why. It must be 50°C, and there's no shade at all. It is impossible to enjoy it. We walk along a sandy track up and down hills for ten minutes looking at the petrified trees, hard solid things, getting through a litre bottle of water in quick thirsty gulps.

'What exactly is a petrified forest anyway?' I ask Geoffrey, who had his nose buried in the guidebook the night before. These stumps certainly look as though they have been petrified—they look like rocks with bits of granite in them—but how?

'In ancient times Lesbos had many active volcanoes and the area was covered with pine and beech trees as well as palm trees,' Geoffrey says. 'We are talking twenty million years ago.' He produces the guidebook. 'The formation of the Petrified Forest is a result of the intense volcanic activity during late Oligocene–Middle Miocene ... whatever the hell that means.' (That last bit wasn't written in the guidebook.) 'The volcanic eruptions during this time produced lava and volcanic ash, which covered the vegetation of the area. The rapid covering of tree trunks, branches and leaves led to isolation from atmospheric conditions. Along with the volcanic activity, hot solutions of silicon dioxide penetrated and impregnated the volcanic materials that covered the tree trunks. Then the major fossilisation process started with a molecule by molecule replacement of organic plant by inorganic materials.'

Fair enough I suppose, but it is too bloody hot to stand here listening to this. We scurry back to the information centre, where Geoffrey reads a bit more.

'In the case of the Petrified Forest of Lesvos, the fossilisation was perfect, due to favourable fossilisation conditions. Characteristics of the tree trunks such as the annual rings, barkers, as well as the internal structure of the wood are all preserved in excellent condition.'

I'm impressed. Despite the heat, it had been an eerie feeling to be close to such a geological phenomenon.

I ask the man behind the counter why they don't plant trees in the valley so tourists can enjoy walking around the exhibits in a little comfort.

'Nothing would grow in that valley,' he tells us, and recommends we go to nearby Sigri, where there is an air-conditioned museum with so much information about the Petrified Forest we will be forever relieved of our ignorance.

So we go.

Sigri is a little coastal fishing village on the bay with a castle, a wharf, fishermen mending nets, and an agreeably small number of little hotels and villas clustered around a tiny shimmering bay.

We walk up to the castle, an eighteenth-century structure that is now just neglected ruins. We scramble around, but it is obvious from the pungent odour and stains on the crumbling old walls that several hundred men have used this as a convenient place to take a pee. Still, it has fabulous views out over the blue sea, and we stay here admiring the scene for as long as we can stand the smell.

This is indeed a picturesque place. Inviting little restaurants sit on the terraced hills, beckoning us inside with enticing—if badly spelled—blackboard offerings. We have loved the Greek translations of food items into English on menus. We have tried not to laugh at the quirky mistakes—try getting us to translate something from English into Greek and see our mistakes—but they are very engaging.

One restaurant here has 'lobster alive today' and 'home make dishes'. So far in our travels we have perused countless menus outside tavernas (we do like our food), and we've found them all to be exactly the same everywhere—but at least with an entertaining variety of spelling mistakes. We have passed up the 'shrimps in carry' at one charming beachfront place, and haven't had the courage to order cabbage at any place yet, especially the one that listed it on its blackboard as 'garbage'. Boiled grass has appeared on every menu but we haven't been tempted yet, and we didn't know what to make of the item that read simply 'stuffed'.

'Is it stuffed eggplant? Stuffed tomato?' we had asked the waiter, but he shrugged and said, 'No, just stuffed.'

And why not?

We wander Sigri's delightful little streets. This is the kind of place you can imagine great writers living while they write their big novels. You can just see them sitting in a small sunny room in one of these little hotels overlooking the blue bay, tapping out clever words all day and then going down to the tavernas at night to drink retsina and talk with the locals, living semi-reclusively until they finish their novel. It's a romantic thought, and I can just see myself here one day, gazing up from my laptop to look out over the peaceful sea view instead of the bookshelves in my cramped office in Australia.

We continue our wandering and see no-one apart from an old lady in widow's black walking along with a young boy of about two, singing to him. It's a sight we have encountered often in Greece—hunched-over grandmas walking hand in hand with young children, teaching them simple songs or counting numbers.

Finally we come to the Natural Museum of the Lesvos Petrified Forest, a modern building of great impressiveness sitting on top of a hill overlooking the sea. We walk over its glass-tiled floor with petrified bits and forest fragments embedded in it and agree that this is much more comfortable than trying to walk around a valley in 50°C heat.

We sit alone in a small room watching a slide show of the forest we have just been in, with close-up shots of the tree trunks and other fossils. We try to look intelligent and interested, but after looking at two dozen petrified stumps we become bored. In another room we find a cinema showing a re-enactment of how the forest would have looked while it was actually being petrified. This excites us because it's much easier to relate to than a lot of hard stumps. We rush eagerly to the cinema entrance to be told we can't go in because the film is in Greek. We want to demand half our money back but head out huffily instead.

As we step outside into the brutal sunshine I think about my friend Ida Duncan at home in Australia, and how horrified she would be that we didn't spend the entire day in the museum. She would surely have done so herself—and learnt every pedantic detail about fossilisation to repeat to her many friends on her return.

I'll pause here for a minute to tell you about Ida, a woman in her eighties who has more energy, and looks better than, most fifty-year-olds. Her *joie de vivre* is a pleasure to watch, and everyone who meets her envies her capacity to embrace everything she does with so much enthusiasm. She can still thrill like a young woman to the smallest of life's pleasures; she has an endless interest in people; she can recite every line of Australian bush poetry ever written; she is a champion flirt and can get any man to do her bidding even though she has been married to her adoring husband for more than sixty years; and she has a passion for Greek history. She studied it at university when she was a 'mature' student and did a study tour of Greece with a learned professor whom she developed a crush on, much to her dear and patient husband's amusement.

Among her myriad community works, she founded the Noosa Botanical Gardens near where we live. Not content with planting thousands of trees and other exotic plants and creating peaceful gardens for everyone to enjoy, she also built an amphitheatre on a natural hillside in the gardens leading down to a placid lake, all with no government funding and despite considerable protest from a few vocal locals who thought it might be used by graffiti-minded skateboarders. I urge anybody who visits our part of the world to go to the Noosa Botanical Gardens and see this amphitheatre: sit on its curved steps, look down to its circular stage, and up to its soaring columns, and let your imagination wander. It is a replica of the grand Greek theatres, designed by Noosa artist Bill McKay and built with donated bricks and labour. People gasp in surprise and admiration when they walk up the hill and come across this striking Greek structure in the middle of a subtropical setting. We have sat in this theatre and watched many concerts—organised by Ida, of course—and with the moon rising over the backdrop of the lake, it is a scene to bring out goose bumps on the arms and to plant itself in your memory forever.

When I tell Ida about my Greek travels, she asks me what ruins I have explored, which ancient theatres I have sat in, which Greek philosophers have I studied.

'None,' I tell her, and she's horrified.

'Didn't you feel the spirit of Pericles when you were in Athens?' she says.

'No, but I did feel humble and awed and moved at the Acropolis. Will that do?'

'No.'

'And I did study this Pericles fellow a bit. I knew he was a democratic leader responsible for the extensive building program in Athens between the 440s and the 420s BC. I really did.'

She isn't satisfied.

'Pericles was a great and influential leader of Athens' democracy during Greece's age of cultural, artistic and intellectual supremacy,' she says, and gives me a book on Hellenic history and sheets of paper on which she has handwritten copious notes about Socrates and Plato as well as her favourite, Pericles.

'He was a man of great eloquence and courage and honour. He beautified Athens; he was a great soldier and leader. The Greeks were the people who brought us culture and theatre and writing. Everything started with the Greeks.'

Ida loves everything about Greece. She has endless photo albums from her trips there, full of photos of her climbing up the steepest steps, sitting in the amphitheatre of Delphi, even being hauled up in a net basket to the towering sandstone cliffs of Meterora to the monastery on top. I think she was about eighty-two when she did that. She tells stories of Greek gods, and legends and myths, at dinner parties and then takes the entertainment off in an entirely different direction with a recital, complete with different voices for different characters, of every verse of Banjo Paterson's 'The Man From Snowy River'. She's the best raconteur I know and I'd lend her to you for your next dinner party if I didn't want to keep her all to myself.

So when I tell her I'd rather be making forays into Greek tavernas than climbing over ruins, she is, understandably not happy with me.

'Ancient Greece is responsible for the civilisation of man,' she says. 'It is the basis of all learning; it is where we get all our Western learning from. The Greek alphabet still hasn't changed. Everyone learnt from ancient Greece, copied them. Everyone, especially the Romans, stole the ideas from the Greeks. The Greeks started everything.'

She gives me a look of despair … and then says: 'Including wine-making.'

Now that's interesting.

We drive north through more hilly country, past several billion more olive trees, and finally arrive at Petra, a lively tourist spot with a long beach filled with people sunning themselves on deckchairs and swimming in the blue sea. A road separates the beach from a long line of cafés, and the whole scene looks immensely touristy, which depresses us a little but intrigues us a lot. We love to wonder where all these people come from. Is this their annual holiday? Do they have just a short time to be here? Are they regulars? We feel smug that we have weeks to spend here, and stop for lunch at a small café where Geoffrey eats yet another Greek salad while I get stuck into a huge club sandwich with chips—and then start complaining about how fat I'm getting. When we finish, Geoffrey says, 'Do you realise that Molyvos, our destination for today, is just around the corner?'

I do not. I feel stupid stopping for lunch just five minutes from our destination. I cannot wait to get to Molyvos. We have forged a bond with the owner of the Seahorse Hotel, our home for the next few weeks, and feel as though we know him well from our email chats. He has promised us a room right at the front, overlooking the harbour, and we have pored over his website and already decided that the Seahorse Hotel is more than perfect.

And, surprise, surprise, it is.

The tiny harbour in which it sits is like a scene from one of those postcards smug acquaintances send you when they're on holiday in the Greek islands, of a scene so impossibly beautiful it makes you hate them. The harbour is enclosed from the sea by a long stone wall and is filled with an assortment of colourful fishing boats, a few sleek yachts and a lot of little dinghies.

Fishermen mend their nets on the decks of their boats, kids fish from the harbour wall, little boats putter in and out, and surrounding every bit of space around this beautiful harbour are tables and chairs of cafés and tavernas outside old stone buildings. It is small, personal, and utterly bewitching.

Our hotel man is not here—a small disappointment—but his friendly thirty-something son is, and his eyebrows shoot up and he takes quite a leap back as we barge into the reception area shouting, 'We're here, we've arrived, how are you?' We know we are a bit loud but these startled looks are unnerving. But he quickly recovers his composure and calms down and shows us to what is indeed the best room in the hotel, overlooking the harbour. Our balcony is con- nected to that of our neighbour, of course, and I curse loudly, because I can see myself sitting out there for hours in the early evening and I do not want my neighbour almost sitting in my lap. But it is the only downside to this lovely place. We have more than enough space in the newly refurbished room to set up a table for my laptop, even to have a little dance should we feel so inclined. We have a refrigerator, massive wardrobes, plenty of cupboards, a king-sized bed, a television to watch those stupendously bad Greek soap operas on if we like, and light and cleanliness everywhere.

And our bathroom is so large I could go out and get one of the mangy cats prowling the harbour and swing it around in there if I wanted to. Glory be. This is the first time yet that we have been happy with a bathroom—it even has a hair dryer, a luxury we have not come across in Greece so far, which makes us gleeful even though Geoffrey has no hair to dry.

Our floor-to-ceiling French doors open onto the fabulous harbour, and if I really want to be snobbish and not talk to my neighbour out on the balcony I can sit just inside the doors and still have the view. It's perfect.

EXPLORING LESBOS

It seems we have no immediate neighbours, so we sit on our balcony in peace every evening, taking countless photos of the colourful wooden boats chugging in and out of the harbour, of the tanned young men and grizzled old men mending nets alongside energetic boys with fishing rods, and the waiters running about with jugs of wine, bottles of ouzo, and plates of sardines and fried cheese.

Each night a tanned middle-aged man with thick grey hair that stands high up on end over his forehead comes out of one of the elegant stone buildings and walks to the edge of the harbour among the clusters of tables at the café below us. He dips a large bucket on the end of a rope into the water, pulls it up and vigorously throws the water all over his little wooden boat, haphazardly swabbing down its tiny decks. He repeats the process a dozen times, without showing the least concern for people dining nearby who get drenched—and they don't seem to mind the salty bath either. It's a scene of great friendliness.

One fisherman becomes our favourite. He spends hours standing on the decks of his big wooden boat right below us, cigarette in mouth, battered hat on head. He grabs up a handful of fishing net from a messy pile on his left, examines it, occasionally picks out bits of flotsam, and then tosses it to his right until the second pile becomes huge and the original pile is diminished. Then he starts the process over again, going from right to left. He is there every afternoon until late into the evening and we never see him go anywhere.

'That netting is his worry beads,' Geoffrey says. 'He doesn't seem to actually mend the net. He just plays with it.' Perhaps it's therapeutic. It certainly is for us.

We look forward to the early evening routines of the harbour—the shopkeeper next door setting up after siesta, unfurling his blinds, putting out his sign, brushing down the shelves holding his jewellery and sculptures, the woman on the other side arranging her handknitted garments and postcards outside the tiny door of her shop. We worry if one of the tavernas doesn't fill as quickly as the others and watch the owner beckon strolling people to take a table. We become vicariously involved in their businesses, willing customers to make purchases, to keep the Molyvos harbour economy booming for the summer season.

Despite this activity we have been sleeping like dead people, thanks to the double-glazing and the lightproof shutters on our windows. While the action outside clatters through the night, we sleep without stirring inside our dark and soundproof cavern. When we awake in the morning it feels like midnight and we doze again. When we can sleep no more we stagger to the shutters, certain it is still the dead of night, open them and find dazzling sunlight and people preparing for lunch. We join the flurry by the harbour edge for a late breakfast of rolls, croissants, jam, eggs and coffee.

'Is this fabulous or what?' we say, and feed the fish little bits of flaky croissant and bread roll. We rarely get going on our forays until after midday.

Molyvos is a medieval town at the northern tip of Lesbos, clinging to the slopes of the hill. It is topped by its castle, a stunning regal crown built in the Byzantine era which can be seen from the harbour and from many other parts of the town. At night, looking up to the castle's floodlit walls from our favourite waterfront café—run by a pretty woman and her even prettier daughter—we feel old stirrings of romance. One morning we ask the girl at the information centre if there is to be a summer concert in the castle in the next few weeks.

'You just missed one, last Sunday,' she says with the sort of insincere smile that people—usually unpaid volunteers who resent you being on holiday—in tourist information centres all over the world give you when they tell you news that isn't going to please you. 'And there are no more concerts scheduled for at least another month,' she continues, positively grinning now.

We decide to hire a motor scooter and do short trips each day if concerts in castles are clearly out of the question. It is years since I have sat on the back of a motor scooter and even getting my leg over the seat is difficult at first. Hoisting a leg in the air and throwing it over something about waist high has not been part of my exercise regime for the past three decades, and I do not look good as I swing clumsily and lumber laboriously onto the scooter behind Geoffrey. But there is one advantage of being plump and old on a motor scooter—the love handles around Geoffrey's waist. They're perfect to grip onto. As you could guess, he objects at first, but then accepts my hanging onto them, and they make me feel secure as we scoot along.

'Lean over with me,' he says as we round the first tight bend, and he leans over himself, theatrically, I think—he's a show-off sometimes, as most blokes are when they get on a motorbike, even if it is only a small scooter. But I just can't lean. Having my nose lowered to within a few centimetres of the bitumen might have seemed daring thirty years ago, but no amount of his urging can make me lean with him now. He yells at me as I lean dangerously in the opposite direction and almost topple us over.

After a few days I actually do get a little of my confidence back, but I still look with envy at gorgeous young women in shorts and cropped tops sitting helmet-less and casual on the back of the scooters, their backs straight, their slim arms *not* wrapped around their partner's waists (no love handles on the young blokes yet, but let them wait) but reaching down and resting languidly on their own tanned thighs. It's a far different look from mine: a helmet pulled down over my forehead, hunched over, grabbing rolls of blubber, with my face pressed into Geoffrey's back.

Molyvos differs in its architecture from other Greek islands. It has tall stone buildings and houses with timber balconies lining narrow cobbled streets covered in trellises of pale lavender wisteria. These stately buildings climb the mountainside up to the castle, and we wander from the harbour up through the maze of shops and tavernas admiring the enchanting views. There is no denying the town's tourist appeal, but there is an air of naturalness about it, of locals going about their business and, while welcoming visitors, not trying too hard to cash in on them.

We love this mix of working harbour, small town, abundance of cafés and tavernas, and enough history and ruins for when we work up the energy to explore. We are more interested in Greek countryside—with a bit of hedonism thrown in—now that we have the scooter.

'Skala Sikaminias looks good,' I say one morning at breakfast, pointing it out on the map. It's not far from Molyvos, and although it is on the coast, we will have to drive up and over the mountain to get to it, which should make for a perfect little outing.

Yet again we go through gorgeous countryside filled with olive and oleander trees, and look up to red-roofed hilltop towns with views over green valleys. It is so delightful that we make a promise to discover every one of these small places.

We arrive at Sikaminia first, before Skala Sikaminias, a small clustered town of terracotta-tiled houses tumbling down the slopes of Mt Lepetimnos, with green views of pinewood and plane trees immediately below the hills.

Sikaminia is sleepy right now, but we stop in a tiny square, obviously the centre of village life with its tiny supermarket, closed at the moment, and tables and chairs outside its one closed café. The entire square is covered with wisteria and grapevines, but the sunlight comes through, making dappled patterns on the stones; it is utterly charming. We peer through the doors of the supermarket. Actually we're being generous calling it that, as it's no bigger than the average Australian bedroom, but it is crammed with supplies. We have already been in tiny grocery stores in town, some of them so small our backs scraped against the aisle behind us as we examined the shelves in front of us. Meeting someone in the aisle means one of you has to back up and out and makes a simple shopping expedition more interesting.

We have a feeling this square would have been a hive of activity a few hours ago, with old men playing cards at the tables, housewives cramming into the tiny shop, locals chatting as they went about their morning business. But now it is empty.

'We really must get up earlier and enjoy these places in the morning,' I tell Geoffrey, who doesn't answer but leads me up from the square and into a network of narrow stone streets. We look over walls into tiny gardens filled with vegetables, and at small stone houses with enclosed wooden balconies, all with magnificent views down the mountain to the flat blue sea in the distance. There is something very special about this place.

Notices are plastered on telegraph poles everywhere and would no doubt tell us, if we could read Greek, of upcoming local events and interesting community happenings. We climb up the steps in the narrow streets, right to the top of the hill, and sit on big flat rocks and look out to sea while Geoffrey theorises.

'They don't do maintenance here,' he says. 'Look at the rusted tin doors and flaky woodwork. These people give attention to matters of importance, like growing vegetables.'

And that sounds very observant and correct until we get up and walk around to another street, where we find a comprehensive maintenance project being carried out on an old house. In fact it's almost an entire construction, but in keeping with the original stone and wooden architecture. We pass shifty-eyed cats that stare balefully at us and then we sit for a while again. The only sound comes from the cicadas. This is a special place, but we decide we've lingered too long. We walk back down to the tiny square, find a stone fountain built into the wall—it has a gleaming new brass tap, which doesn't help Geoffrey's theory either—drink sweet water from it, hoist ourselves back on the scooter and head off to Skala Sikaminia.

This place looks exactly like the scene you find on postcards depicting Greece at its most charming. It's another working harbour with boats, fishing nets and tavernas full of Greek families. We can see Turkey—mountainous, mysterious, mauve—across the sea.

'Lunch in one of these little places right on the harbour?' I ask Geoffrey.

'Yes, but a swim first,' he says. 'We have to earn these things.'

The beach—only a few minutes' walk away—is rocky and uncomfortable. Getting into the water by slipping and tumbling over wet rocks is very difficult. After falling many times I'm about to give up when other people arrive and have the same problem. A middle-aged man who is already out quite deep, floating contentedly in the clear water, shouts out loud instructions to a woman struggling on the rocks. She looks as lumbering as I do, and although I can't understand a word the man is shouting, it is obvious he's giving instructions on graceful water entering.

The woman tries to follow his insistent coaching and takes cautious steps, but she can't make it, and his shouting becomes so loud that it drives us mad. We give up on attempts to swim and sit under trees on big round concrete things—which we find out later are old olive-pressing stones—to look at the water. Another family group arrives and tries the awkward water-entering thing. This excites our man to scream out urgent instructions again.

'He must be the local Chamber of Commerce man or mayor, or the Greek equivalent,' I comment. 'He looks as though he's the authority on all things in this village.' He reminds us of Bill with the binoculars at the Natural History Collection in Vatera. After he eventually sees the family safely in the water he gets out confidently without a single slip or stumble, and wanders back, still in his swimsuit and dripping water, towards the small harbour. He stops on the way to give vociferous instructions, including much hearty arm waving, to a group approaching the beach. Every town should have a man like this.

We wander back ourselves, stopping at an old disused olive oil factory, Geoffrey doing that man thing again, knocking on the old wooden gates to test for woodworm or olive worm I suppose. We see more of the old concrete olive-pressing things and signs of a factory that was once productive, but is now closed. It interests us for a few minutes, but lunch is beckoning at one of the small waterfront places.

We choose the one with an enticing blackboard special of the day of a mixed grilled seafood plate for two, a Greek salad, tzatziki, bread and half a litre of wine for 14 euros, and sit so close to the water we can see the fish gliding just beneath the surface.

We're surrounded by Greek people of all ages eating and drinking, without an English-speaking person in sight. The waiters rush in and out of the kitchen, throwing leftover bread and fish heads into the water, fishing boats bob on the calm water, fishermen sort out their nets, hungry cats hover beneath tables waiting for titbits, a dog wanders past, squats, wees, moves on, another waiter boots the cats gently out of his way and throws the last contents of someone's water jug into the harbour. We relax completely and feed the cats the fish heads from our small fish.

As we are finishing our meal with great sighs of contentment, our Chamber of Commerce man, now out of his swimsuit and smartly dressed in a clean shirt and long pants, his moustache and hair combed neatly, strides authoritatively by. Uninvited, he pulls out a chair at the table of an old couple near us and starts shouting at them, no doubt telling them how to eat. But they look quite happy to receive his unasked for intrusion and get on with their lunch, mostly ignoring him.

It's been a lovely afternoon, visiting the quiet hilltop town and lunching in the pretty harbour, and we thrill to the knowledge that there are so many more small places like this so close by.

'We really are very fortunate,' I tell Geoffrey as I hoist my leg awkwardly over the bike and grab for those comforting love handles once again.

DONKEY TREKKING

We haven't seen much of our hotel owner—the man we bonded with over the emails—perhaps because he is on duty in the mornings and we have yet to make it up before midday. His son runs the hotel in the afternoon and tends to all our needs, most of which involve borrowing paperbacks and buying the English newspapers. Reading has become another indulgence. Lazy mornings with Bryce Courtenay or Wilbur Smith, or English tabloids, are as indulgent as this holiday itself. Working as a feature writer for a newspaper in Australia myself, I read these papers with a writer's eye, and if I may be bold enough to say so, I think our Australian journalism is every bit as good as the English. And we don't seem to have bitchy columnists writing spiteful pieces about tall poppies and celebrities, as the English do. The journalists have their arrows drawn at a big-breasted English beauty called Jordan at the moment. They call her a dumb bimbo with no talent other than to get photographed at parties (which is pretty much a talent to be admired, in my opinion). The English journalists also don't seem to mind dressing up and posing as bogus deliverymen and plastic surgeons among other things, in pursuit of a story. One actually got inside Windsor Castle to expose the appalling lack of security there, and then bragged about his underhanded operations on the front page, running his own photo standing outside the castle. Another journalist rented rooms in Harley Street, gave himself impressive fake credentials, had a name plate made up with false letters after his name, and put an advertisement for botox injections and liposuction treatments in the paper and waited for the telephone inquiries to pour in—which they did—so he could boast about how easy it was to set yourself up as a plastic surgeon and take people's money to puff up their lips and suck out their fat when the only qualifications you really had were for tapping out words on a keyboard. It seems an awful lot of sneakiness to get a story, but who am I to criticise?

This morning we have seen a brochure in the hotel's reception area for a sunset donkey trek. It sounds touristy, but I am in the mood for small adventures of the donkey kind so I encourage Geoffrey.

'Look, it says we trek along the back roads through dramatic scenery to the beach at Eftalou where our guide will make a beach barbecue for us,' I say. 'It sounds all right, let's do it.'

Geoffrey is not so sure, but he agrees to go along with it because we have sat on our balcony for far too long and not ventured anywhere near enough to other wonders on this beautiful island.

'We'd better take something to drink because I doubt the guide's beach barbecue will include wine,' Geoffrey the Thoughtful says.

'We can't very well take a bottle of wine if no-one else in the group has any,' I remind him, so we decide on gin instead, and pour it into an empty water bottle to ensure no-one will know we are desperate pisspots.

We are late at our donkey meeting point. We set off on the scooter in time to meet the donkey guide but my watch is slow, and the group has left without us. Determined by this stage to do this donkey trek— and not just because we have paid 28 non-refundable euros for the pleasure—we ask directions at a nearby café and the owner tells us the group has not long left and the donkey farm, where they will be saddling up right now, is just down the road. We can catch them if we hurry.

Who would have thought that now, as a woman of advancing years, I would be racing on the back of a motor scooter along a back road on a Greek island chasing donkeys? But there you go. You never know what life has in store for you.

Fortunately, we catch the group just as they are about to leave. They are all sitting calmly on their donkeys side-saddle, as we arrive stressed and anxious. The guide, a brown and weathered Greek man with muscles like Popeye in tanned arms protruding from a sleeveless T-shirt, and thick strong jeans-encased legs plugged into brown leather boots, says nothing to us as we babble our apologies. He goes to get another two donkeys from a wooden hut at the back of the enclosure while everyone else looks at us with ill-concealed annoyance. People who hold up others in groups on tours or buses are the worst kind of travellers; normally we are the ones doing the glaring, so we say sorry a dozen times to every person on every donkey until the guide appears with two docile beasts and leads them over to us. He takes one appraising look at me and obviously decides my donkey will not support my weight.

God, the embarrassment, as he gets a slim woman to dismount from her donkey and take mine, and gives me her bigger, stronger one. Even Geoffrey's donkey appears smaller than mine and Geoffrey is a good 10 kilograms heavier than me.

Everyone, now impatient to get going, sits silently and watches as I try to heave myself up onto my donkey. If I was embarrassed before, I am now a lather of humiliation. The guide shouts at me to put one of my feet into his strong hands, and the poor man takes all my weight as I heave myself up in such an ungraceful manner everyone turns their eyes away in sympathy. It takes three attempts and much shouting from the guide before I finally mount the beast (the donkey, not the guide). I don't know why we are to sit side-saddle, even the blokes—we all look bit girlie—but we're finally ready, and at last we take off in an untidy posse.

We all appear to be donkey virgins, and can't seem to steer the beasts in the right direction. We are on a bitumen road, and while there is not much traffic, there are some cars and motor scooters trying to pass us and it could be dangerous. Our guide, sitting handsomely on top of a strong brown horse himself, ties a blue checked tea towel around his head in Lawrence of Arabia style and tries to tidy up the straggling herd. He berates us sternly.

'Keep to the right,' he shouts, and we pull on our ropes to try to keep the donkeys to the right. Our group is a mixed bunch of all ages and nationalities, and I am delighted to say, I am not the stoutest person here. An English woman wearing bright lime green pants almost identical to my own has a large posterior and it's hanging outstandingly over the side of her donkey. Yet even so, her donkey seems to canter along briskly, as though carrying the lightest of ballerinas, while mine struggles to manage a slow clip clop.

'Is my bum as big as hers?' I mouth discreetly to Geoffrey, with a bit of eye rolling in her direction when he turns back to look at me, because by now I am trailing behind everyone else. He can't understand me, which is just as well; it's a rude and stupid question.

Finally we turn off the main road onto a rough track. It's about seven-thirty in the evening now and very peaceful. As I gain confidence, I feel secure enough to loosen my tight grip on the reins and take a look around. The evening sun's soft colours play on the surrounding mountains, turning them pale gold and light green; the air is still and the clumps of wild oregano by the side of the track smell fresh and herby. We pass goats, their beards ruffling in the light breeze, and they stop their grass munching for a minute to look at us—there is equal curiosity on both sides.

We are all getting the hang of this donkey steering by now and people are relaxing, laughing and talking to each other. I am still at the rear. Donkey Man shouts out both encouragement and admonishment to his donkeys, in a deep voice. They all have names: the leader is Poppy, mine is Rebecca, Geoffrey's is Olga.

Rebecca tires even further beneath my weight and lags behind despite my cheerful urgings. Donkey Man has to constantly drop back from the group to give her encouragement.

But the attention is not all on me. Poppy, up the front, is a bit of a wanton lass. She wants to go her own way, and to make it worse, her rider, a lanky middle-aged Dutchman, is quite the stirrer. He keeps giving Poppy instructions in Dutch—to go faster, I think—but this is a Greek donkey, used to her own language, and she's having none of it. She wants to stop and eat the sweet green grass growing by the track.

Donkey Man gets cross and tells us all not to give our own instructions to the donkeys.

'They listen only to me; don't speak to them,' he shouts. By now several donkeys can't resist the green growth along the road and stop to munch.

Suddenly Rebecca perks up beneath me. Her ears stiffen, her nose twitches, and her head lifts up. She seems to smell something in the air, and it's giving her a new sense of purpose. Then I smell it too, and I'm horrified. It's the gin from my water bottle. The top mustn't be on properly, and I can tell by the strong and unmistakable alcoholic smell that it's leaking copiously inside my backpack—both Rebecca and I will soon be engulfed in a gin fog. She takes off with gusto, and bumps into the other donkeys in her haste to get to the front of the group.

Well, if it takes a drop of gin to revive her I am not going to complain. We take the lead now, much to the Dutchman's annoyance, and I reach awkwardly to my pack to secure the lid on the gin bottle.

We canter down onto a narrow pebbled path by the edge of a beach, the donkeys' hoofs sure and confident on the difficult terrain. The sun is shining on the blue water and it is as serene and magical as you could imagine. Then we come up from the beach back onto the bitumen road, and pass resort-style hotels with inviting blue swimming pools where tanned people still sit sunning themselves. As we pass they get up and rush to the road to take pictures of us. I have never been a tourist attraction before, so I wave merrily at them and pose for their cameras.

Donkeys are lovely beasts of burden if you have ever stopped to think about them. What marvellous, patient, strong animals they are—anyone who can bear my bulk for an hour has my admiration for life.

By now we really all do have the hang of this donkey riding and we've all settled down, apart from a couple of teenage English girls who screech at each other incessantly until we arrive at the beach of Eftalou. It is quiet now on the beach and the lowering sun is turning the waters deep blues and hazy mauves.

Poppy stops to munch the grass again, and it infuriates Donkey Man who screams at her.

'Poppy, I get an aching throat just talking to you.'

But Poppy pays no attention and continues to munch.

The rest of us tie our donkeys up on a long rope at the top of a hill looking down on the beach and then hike down to the water's edge. We are at the most northern part of Lesbos and can see Turkey just five kilometres across the sea.

Donkey Man tells us that an American woman once swam from Turkey to Greece just to prove a point, but warns us never to attempt it ourselves as it is, of course, illegal.

'Many refugees have tried to do this and drowned. It is very sad,' he says, not looking in the least sad. He's still looking up at Poppy and the lanky Dutchman, who is now tying her up with the rest of the donkeys. An attractive English woman—Donkey Man's business partner, we find out later—is waiting for us on the beach with modest preparations for our barbecue. She greets us, pushing a few rocks side by side for seats.

So now it's time to relax and I've lost half the gin from my water bottle. Geoffrey is in the mood for a drink, and while there is enough left for a sneaky swig, we feel guilty in front of the others. We are saved by Donkey Man, who points to a large plastic olive oil bottle sitting on the sand next to a couple of bottles of water and a few cans of Sprite.

'That's the bar,' he says. 'Help yourselves.'

White wine, as rough as it gets, is in the olive oil bottle; the attractive English woman produces small plastic cups and we all sniff at the olive oil bottle warily and screw up our noses, but still accept a taste. After the first cautious sip, it tastes like nectar in the fabulous surroundings of the small cove. By now the sun has changed the sea to orange, purple, deep blue. It is still very warm and there is no-one on the beach except our little group. Donkey Man has an old rusty deep freeze cabinet thing—something that would look very much at home on top of a rubbish tip—near the rocks in a corner of the cove. He produces big bags of pork ribs, containers of salad and loaves of bread from it. He burrows down into it again to pull out another olive oil bottle filled with more wine, and then reaches down again for logs of wood and an axe. He chops firewood, the muscles bulging in his strong arms, his tea towel headgear flapping rakishly. This is one tough bloke, and although my first impression of him was that he was a big boof-head, I can see now that he is a smart and wily dude. I think I fancy him. Especially when he shouts at me.

The lanky Dutchman has taken on the role of barman while we wait for the fire to turn to hot embers. He refills our plastic cups over and over, draining the dregs from the olive oil bottles.

'There's plenty more,' Donkey Man says, now from a prone position on the beach, balancing his plastic cup of wine on his chest, and the Dutchman rushes over to the rusty cabinet and produces yet another olive oil bottle. We are all enjoying this tremendously now. A few people have their swimsuits on and are frolicking in the water. I keep edging towards the woman in the lime green pants to stand next to her so Geoffrey can compare our bottoms and give me a favourable answer to my previous question.

'Bigger than yours, definitely,' Geoffrey says generously, because he's on his fifth cup of wine now.

The sun becomes a bright orange ball as it starts to sink in the sky, which causes everyone to abandon their wine cups for a moment and reach for cameras. It is a gorgeous scene—if you don't believe me, just look on my website at one of the many photos we took of the sinking sun turning the water pink, blue, orange and red, look at the transparent spume on the waves, see the silhouette of the rocks against the skyline.

Donkey Man seems in no hurry to get the pork cooking, which suits us, as the wine has oiled the tongues of all the goup, and we chat like old friends.

The English lady in the lime pants and her husband tell me about the extortionate house prices in the UK. They are keen to hear about Australia, because apart from watching *Neighbours* and reading all the gossip about Kylie Minogue, they don't hear much on their news about Australia.

'The only time Australia was in the news was when your Prime Minister wouldn't let that boatload of refugees land,' the guy tells me.

'Yes, I know,' I say, feeling ashamed. But then.

'We applauded him so much. We wish our Prime Minister would take such a stand. We thought yours was brave, and we loved it.'

Then we talk about the refugee problem in the UK and I do feel proud of our country.

'We'd love to come to Australia to visit, but don't you Aussies call us all whingeing Poms?' the man says.

'No, no,' I shout, just a bit too loudly. 'At least not any more. It's not politically correct, or it's racist or something. We're not allowed to.'

This seems to please him immensely, and I think he went home to the UK and immediately made plans to sell his family home and lucrative business, uproot his kids from school, leave his ailing parents and emigrate to Australia. All thanks to me.

Another thirty minutes and two hundred photos of the setting sun later, Donkey Man decides to put the pork on the barbecue, which is actually a bit of old grill resting precariously over the embers. We all gather around the fire, as people do when meat is cooking, to look at it, have a poke at it and turn it, until finally it's ready and we line up with paper plates for long strips of pink, succulent and perfectly cooked pork with just enough crunchy fat to dribble down chins. Everyone stops talking for a while.

With the Greek salad and the bread and the cheap wine and the glorious setting, it's the best meal I've had in many years.

'This meat is delicious, absolutely beautiful,' I tell Donkey Man sincerely.

'I know,' he says and takes another swig of wine. I am a little scared of him.

'Do all your donkeys have names?' I ask him.

'Every one of them, and they all know their names,' he says and flicks back his tea towel as though it is a lock of long hair. I definitely have a crush on him.

'I have thirty donkeys in total,' he says.

'Are they working donkeys or tourism donkeys?'

'I never work my donkeys apart from this,' he says angrily. My crush grows.

'Well, they are strong if they can take my weight,' I say.

This brings forth a snort of derision from our man, and he calls for another top-up of his wine cup. The Dutchman comes running over with the olive oil bottle. 'My donkeys can take up to two hundred kilos.'

That makes me feel better.

'Some of the donkeys on the island work hard, especially at olive-picking time,' he says. 'They have to carry heavy baskets full of olives. Mine rest at olive-picking time. Mine are just for these treks.'

He dismisses me then to talk to one of the young girls, and I slope off to watch jealously. The lanky Dutchman, obviously a raconteur as well as a stirrer, starts to tell stories. Nobody listens, so he starts to sing English songs. What is it with these Northern Europe people? They sing at the drop of a donkey dropping and seem to know all the English words to songs we wouldn't be caught dead singing, even at our drunkest.

'It's a long way to Tipperary,' he sings in a deep and melodious voice. 'It's a long way to go.'

All right. No-one we know is here and we will never see these people again. We join in.

'What Shall We Do with the Drunken Sailor' he launches into next. You don't believe me, do you? A Dutchman on a small beach on an island called Lesbos singing 'What Shall We Do with the Drunken Sailor'? But it's true.

We all sing along as the sun finally sinks into the sea and the lights of Turkey start to twinkle across the water.

'Show Me The Way To Go Home', the Dutchman sings and no-one but me seems to see the absurdity of singing such a ridiculous song in such a glorious setting, and everyone joins in, except Donkey Man. He remains aloof, watching, sipping his wine, until suddenly he leaps up from the sand, throws down his wine cup and points to the Dutchman.

'Are you crazy? As crazy as me?' he challenges.

'Of course,' is the reply, which is fair enough. Anyone singing 'What Shall We Do with the Drunken Sailor' couldn't help but make such an admission.

'Are you crazy? You? You? You?' Donkey Man points to all the other men, and they all agree that yes, there is a little craziness in them, along with half a litre of rough wine.

'Then follow me,' Donkey Man says and leads them down to the end of the small beach, a few dozen metres away from us women.

There he rips off his clothes quickly and plunges into the sea, urging them to follow with imperative shouts, much like the ones he gives his donkeys. There is hesitation from everyone except the Dutchman, who pulls off his shorts and undies, throws off his shirt, shucks his sandals and is in the water in seconds. Soon the others follow; the women giggle as flashes of white buttocks rush before us. In five minutes all the men are in the water, laughing and yelping with pleasure. The women are jealous.

'Take your clothes off, come in,' Donkey Man shouts to us, but no-one takes up his offer.

After ten minutes the men cautiously come out, hands covering modesty, for now the moon is bright and the night is clear. The

Dutchman's wife can't resist. She wanders over for a closer look as more men emerge from the water.

'The water is obviously very cold,' she shouts back to us, and we all laugh hysterically and pass the olive oil bottle around again.

Back the men come to our bit of beach, dressed, refreshed, excited like little boys, and unforunately it is time to go.

'Can the donkeys see in the dark?' I ask Donkey Man, stupidly.

He gives another snort of disdain. 'If not I give them glasses,' he says, and helps us all back up the hill and onto the donkeys.

I am even clumsier than before—nothing to do with the wine, of course—and can't make the leap up to get my bum on side-saddle. Everyone watches, but by this time there is enough wine sloshing inside all our bellies for no-one to care.

We take off drunkenly, Donkey Man shouting at his donkeys, now adding a few colourful words of encouragement.

'You make me go crazy,' he hollers at them. 'Slow down, you fooking donkeys.'

We canter clumsily on in the dark.

'The Wheels of the Bus Go Round and Round,' sings the Dutchman up front.

'Shut the fook up,' I call out, but not too loudly as I am a coward by nature and I really don't want him to hear me.

'Rawhide, Rawhide, Rawhide,' the Dutchman belts out into the night. He really does have the most wonderful baritone voice, but it excites the donkeys into a frenzy.

They go crazy and start to gallop. I almost slip off the saddle and scream girlishly, which incenses Donkey Man.

'Don't make stupid noises to the donkeys,' he shouts at me, and I realise what a baby I am and shut up and hang on for dear life.

Donkey Man gallops on his horse to the front of the posse, his tea towel streaming raffishly behind him, his neat round buttocks high up off the saddle, his reins thrashing the horse's side. My crush turns to something less wholesome.

He tells the Dutchman off angrily, much to the relief of everyone.

'I am the only one who gives fooking instructions to the fooking donkeys,' he shouts, and the Dutchman finally shuts up.

We canter back to the donkey farm in boozy solidarity after that, the donkeys' hoofs making a pleasant rhythmic clopping sound on the bitumen in the quiet night. It is now about ten in the evening, a beautiful clear warm night, and as we come closer to Molyvos, we can see the castle magnificently lit up, its ancient walls so spectacular we can't take our eyes off them. The lights of Molyvos twinkle before us, guiding us back, and it is memorable; as beautiful a scene as we have yet experienced.

It is obvious, by the sweet murmurings everyone is making in their donkeys' ears, that we have all become attached to our donkeys. Personally, I am wine-soaked sad at the thought of saying goodbye to Rebecca. She's been a hero, carrying me silently, stoically, for two hours. Geoffrey is looking misty-eyed at saying farewell to Olga, too. The only one who looks relieved is Donkey Man, as he takes off saddles and leads his beasts back into their enclosure.

'And you thought that was going to be an awful touristy excursion,' I say to Geoffrey as we close our shutters on the harbour activity an hour later, preparing for another coma-like sleep in our dark cave.

'Yes. But so did you,' he answers. 'And don't think I didn't notice you eyeing off that donkey man like a pre-pubescent schoolgirl.'

EXPLORING GREEK CUISINE

We have made it our business to patronise every one of the tavernas in the Molyvos harbour outside our hotel. It's our duty. The one next door to our hotel is run by a Greek Australian man. Actually, so many Greeks have lived in Australia for some time. Many who emigrated to Australia in the 1950s and 1960s and lived most of their working lives there have now retired back to Greece. This is exactly the story of our host tonight.

He says his Australian name is Ian and he spent fifteen years in Melbourne and only left when Melbourne went through that depressing time during the Cain and Kirner governments in the early 1990s. Ian loved Melbourne before then and still goes back for holidays, but can't recognise the place now. His brother, who lives here in Molyvos, convinced him to come home and buy this restaurant, and now he works only a few months a year and does nothing at all during the winter.

While we eat a big baked potato with garlic and olive oil, shrimp and fetta in a spicy tomato sauce, fresh mixed vegetables (from a can) and pieces of pork with potatoes and onion, Ian pulls up a chair and tells us of his early years in Australia.

'The Greeks did all the jobs Australians wouldn't do,' he says. 'We worked all hours in the milk bars and fish and chip shops. All Melbourne's milk bars were owned by Greeks. Now when I visit Melbourne I can see it has gone to the dogs. Too many migrants. Too many Vietnamese and Chinese. I don't like them.'

We dip our heads to our pork and potato and onion to hide our smiles.

'They are ruining Melbourne with their funny food and strange habits,' he says, and we can't let that go.

'But that was how Australians felt about you Greeks in the 1950s and 1960s, when you went to live there.'

'That was different,' he replies, which of course to his mind it was, and I'm sure it won't be too long before the Vietnamese and Chinese are saying the same thing about the Afghans and the Iranians.

The next day we lunch at the café around the corner from our hotel beneath strings of sun-drying octopus legs dotted with brown suckers. They are tied at the top of their legs with little noose-like loops on one long piece of string that runs from one end of the café to the other, and they dance a merry jig in the breeze. What our chicken salad lacks in taste, the surroundings oversupply in prettiness.

Back at the hotel we have neighbours now and have to share our balcony space, which causes me to throw hissy fits every evening at our sitting time. But our neighbours obviously dislike this space sharing as much as I do, because each time I venture my nose out the door they rush inside. We take turns. If I see them really enjoying themselves on the balcony I stay just inside the doors, out of sight. When I think they've had enough pleasure I step boldly outside and they run inside. If playing musical balconies means we all get what we want, so be it.

The café directly below us has vast canvas blinds that reach out from the building to the harbour edge to protect customers from the brutal sun. Each night when the sun disappears, someone pulls the giant blinds back, which reveals me sitting there, legs up on the railings, fresh from the shower in my hot pink sarong, often knickerless. Should the unfortunate people below happen to turn their faces upwards, they would never again return to this café, or indeed to the island of Lesbos. But fortunately they don't, which saves me running inside to don underpants, and I linger in this position until dusk every night.

One of the young waiters down in the café has one of those haircuts where his head is shaved all around except for the top bit, which grows thick and flat. From the ground he looks modern and up-to-the-minute groovy; from up here it looks as though he has a cowpat on top of his head. This amuses me each night as much as the net-inspecting man with the cigarette and battered hat amuses Geoffrey. You have to agree, we are simple-minded folks, easily pleased by nothing more than the harbour theatre.

Another night we eat sardines (dry, awful) a baked potato (with cheese and ham, ugh) a kebab (with soggy, stale chips) and fried eggplant (good but oily) at another of the harbourside cafés. When the obliging young waiter comes over and says 'Everything okay?' we chorus, 'Yes, wonderful, just wonderful', and make faces when he's gone. But we eat everything anyway because it is better than my own cooking at home. When he clears our plates and says, 'Wow, you really enjoyed that, didn't you?' we nod enthusiastically and rant on about how good it was. Add 'liar' to 'shallow and judgmental'.

Another night when we sit in yet another restaurant eating yet more Greek salads and tiny fish, the big party boat we have seen tied up during the day sails right up close to our harbour, its lights twinkling more brightly than those on the Christmas tree in Times Square. We can hear the Greek music, see the people dancing on the decks. It sits at the entrance to our harbour for fifteen tantalising minutes, teasing us with its fabulous party sounds. We can see arms on shoulders, Zorba style, and hear the singing ... then it sails out again, twinkling and glimmering merrily, making everyone on shore yearn to be there. It's funny how you can be sitting in a place doing something gorgeous yourself, and still something else across the road, or the water in this case, always seems better. It's a curse I suffer particularly badly from. While I am at a glamorous party I'm worried that I might be missing out on an even better one somewhere else. And don't someone else's party noises always sound so thrilling? A glimpse into a brightly lit home on your way home from some ordinary outing can fill you with longing to be part of the action, to be part of the in crowd, but when you are actually on the inner, the outer (your own home and privacy) always seems more appealing.

I really must inquire about therapy.

We finally visit the castle which has stood guard over us on top of the hill throughout these past weeks. Built in the Byzantine period, it is the best-preserved fortress on Lesbos. We pay the usual few euros to go in, and find ourselves alone as we scramble over a boardwalk and look through the turrets and down to the theatre pit; it is filled with chairs, all facing a dais where summer concerts are held—but not, alas, for us.

Each monument, church or museum we have toured so far—apart from the Acropolis in Athens—has been virtually empty. We are obviously not the only tourists in Greece this year who are not inclined to explore history, castles and ruins. We struggle on, though, spending a contented hour in the castle, admiring the views, getting our money's worth, and then with a 'Well-that's-the-castle-done-then' shrug of the shoulders, we nick off back down to the harbour for more food and drink.

All the restaurants write 'fishes' on their menus. It's very appealing. In one place we laughed out loud at a menu mistake, but the next day couldn't remember what it was. Something to do with the second carafe of wine we ordered in a moment of greedy stupidity.

'What was that menu mistake about fish last night?' I ask Geoffrey in the morning.

He thinks hard for a while but can't recall, maybe because of the third ouzo he ordered, in a moment of *really* greedy stupidity.

'It was about the fish of the day,' I prompt. 'Something about the fish you get when you don't know what the fish you are actually going to get is.'

'Yes, I think I remember now,' he says. 'Something like "unpretentious" fish.'

'No, no, not unpretentious. How could fish be unpretentious?' We both frown and think hard.

'Uninhibited fish?' he tries again.

'No. No.'

'Promiscuous fish?'

He is getting right into this now. He tries again. 'Sexy fish? Wanton fish?'

'No, but something quirky like that.'

'Slutty fish? Follow-me-home-and-fuck-me fish?'

He needs therapy as much as I do.

We can't put it out of our minds, so we revisit that taverna the next night. And there it is on the verbose menu, buried between the 'gardener's salad' and the 'tunny fish salad'—'fish without explanation'.

And really, when you think about it, if you want to describe in advance whatever the fisherman might bring in that day, it is the perfect explanation, isn't it?

We keep putting off our visit to the hot springs at Eftalou due to nothing more than laziness and the knowledge that we have time without measure to visit everything on Lesbos.

One day we get on our scooter and head to the old town of Lafionas, another little village up in the hills behind Molyvos that feels as though the outside world has never touched it. Well, that isn't entirely true. All the old stone houses have green beans and red tomatoes growing in the front gardens, but they also have television aerials and satellite dishes on their roofs. However, the feeling in the narrow cobblestoned streets is definitely one of going back in time, especially as we have arrived again at our usual just-past-midday-and-everyone-is-resting time.

Lafionas is about 200 metres up in the mountains, and as we walk its quiet steep streets we wonder how the locals manage here. Just walking from your front gate to your neighbour's front gate requires an exerting head-down-bottom-up effort. Some of the streets are so steep we feel might fall over when we come back down.

We pass a big new building, evidence of some modernisation, but it is built in the same style as the old buildings, and is so bright and shiny new that it stands out like the proverbial dog's thingies. Most of the houses are tiny. Some have new French-polished doors and shutters, but all in the old stone look. Their front doors open onto the street, and many have the smallest, most adorable courtyards at the front covered in by huge flowering hydrangea bushes that give shade and privacy—except from us, who peer rudely in. We pass an old woman coming out of her vegie garden with three glossy purple eggplants in her arms. She smiles and says 'Geiasas', which we take to mean 'hello' and say it back. We come to a butcher's shop, empty now but for the enormous chopping block, like the cut-off trunk of some monstrously huge tree, sitting in the middle of his shop. That and a big butcher's hook hanging from the roof are the only signs that it is functional, apart from a motor scooter propped against the butcher's block.

At the end of each narrow street we arrive at another crest and look down to the town and coast of Molyvos. It is a tranquil and picturesque scene and we can't understand why more tourists do not leave the beaches and come up here to explore these old villages. But just at this moment we are grateful that they don't. We stop for a long while to look down the mountain across the tops of olive trees.

'What would we all do without the olive?' I say to Geoffrey. 'What sustenance, comfort and wealth has it brought man through the ages. Not to mention the long life it will give us all now that we know all about its health-giving qualities and have banished butter from our diets.'

He doesn't answer. He's spied a big fig tree heavy with figs and he's plucking and eating. He is a nature boy; he likes eating things straight from the trees or ground.

We climb up more narrow streets, looking for Saint Alexandros, tantalisingly signed at each turn. But we can't find it.

'What the hell is it, anyway?' I ask. 'A church? A statue? Is it worth this climb?'

No answer again—there's wild rosemary by the side of the road and Geoffrey is feasting.

We pass goats sitting in the shade of a sprawling fig tree, switching their tails, staring at us. We smell something ripe and powerful, and the ever-observant Geoffrey spies a pig in a pen high on the hill above us. I don't think I have ever seen such a huge pig; it looks more like a baby elephant, apart from its curly tail and big pink snout. It reminds me of something and I can't quite think what. Later, it comes to me: me, in my pink sarong, bending over to give myself a pedicure. (Don't laugh; I have actually seen this image because Geoffrey sneakily photographed me from behind once while I was in mid-pedicure. I have not managed to get him back yet, but I will.)

It smells so overpowering that we don't want to go any further looking for Saint Alexandros, whatever it is, so we wander back down. As we walk, we hear a man's booming voice on a loudspeaker announcing the arrival of the watermelon truck. We have seen this open-back small van before, piled to overflowing with huge watermelons, the loudspeaker on top of its cabin calling out loud urgings to come and taste his lovely melons. All at once the sleepy town comes awake.

Old ladies with scarves around their heads and faces—protection from the sun, or modesty?—burst out of their houses and run down the street, and the shouting and squabbling is joyous as people weigh watermelons on a set of grand and old-fashioned scales attached to the back of the truck. It's a marvellous picture in a lovely old town, so we take a marvellous picture, me worrying that we are intruding on the domestic privacy of these old people. But they wave and smile and say '*Geiasas*' and pose for our camera.

We've had yet another rewarding day and we retire to our hotel room to do the musical chairs on the balcony thing once again with our neighbours. When they finally go out to dinner and leave us, we go back to our harbour watching and book reading. I am right into Bryce Courtenay's *Four Fires* at the moment and loving every word of it. Bryce Courtenay is quite a man. He didn't start writing until he was fifty-five and now has fourteen bestsellers and untold millions of dollars in his bank account. I interviewed him once on the telephone—I know, I know, I'm name-dropping—but hey, I can. He is not only a master storyteller, but also a master of the public relations exercise. He was promoting his latest book at the time, *Matthew Flinders' Cat*, and I doubt I have ever spoken to a more charming man. He kept calling me Ann, which isn't so unusual seeing it is my name, but the fact that he remembered it and used it so often was impressive. He said it at the end of each sentence, and we had a fascinating twenty-minute chat, him giving me his utmost attention, answering my questions smoothly, always starting and finishing his answers with Ann. Two days later his publicist rang me to ask why I had not done the interview.

'But I did,' I said. 'We had a terrific chat.'

'Oh, he doesn't remember speaking to you,' she said.

But hey, I am not criticising. Doing a dozen or more interviews a day must be taxing. How could you possibly remember every interviewer's name? But he did make me feel very special at the time.

And I love his books.

HOT SPRINGS
AT EFTALOU

The English newspapers this morning have particularly juicy news.
Lady Mary Archer has had the lid lifted on her secret facelift by a for-
mer employee, whom she is now suing. And that cheating army major
Charles Ingram, who tried to dupe *Who Wants To Be A Millionaire?* by
having his wife cough out the answers, has agreed to resign from the
army and fall on his sword, but will retire on a hefty pension, which
has outraged all of England. Then there's the man convicted for life for
murdering his friend, cutting him up, leaving his head on the front
lawn and roasting his arm in the oven for dinner. This is my favourite,
I think. Or is it the mother of a woman, now sadly dead, who is suing
a hotel in England for negligence because a hot water system in the
room above her daughter's bed burst and fell through the floor, sending 50 gallons of boiling water cascading into the room? The mother
said, 'I'm a bit bitter; I am going to sue.' *A bit bitter?* The marvel of the
British understatement. But what a ghastly accident. I bet the mother

won't ever check into a hotel room herself now without inspecting the room above first.

We go back to Petra. It is just a few minutes by scooter from Molyvos, but we haven't bothered to visit it since we stopped there for lunch that first day just before we arrived. Petra, which means rock in Greek, is an old village with a long esplanade of tourist strip along the beach, but with charming narrow streets behind the front. Looming over the village is a huge perpendicular rock that looks as though it has fallen from the sky, on top of which sits the church of Panagia Glykofiloussa (Our Lady of the Sweet Kiss), built in 1747. It features on all the Lesbos postcards and therefore has to feature on our 'must do' list.

It takes us a long time to find the street leading to the steps up to the church because of the maze of alleyways, but we have come to see the church, and see it we will. I don't know what it is about tourists and churches: why do we feel compelled to go and look in them when we rarely step inside one at home? We pass many intriguing little cafés on the way, tables and chairs outside small holes in the walls in the narrow streets, owners beckoning us to come in once we have finished with the church.

'Go look, but come back here for my fresh meatballs, the best in Petra,' one man says. And another tells us he has the most authentic moussaka on the island. We've actually been yearning for an Asian stir-fry, but there is no hope of finding such a thing here.

We climb the steps to the church and read the signs forbidding me to go in with bare legs, so I wrap my sarong around my shorts and step inside. This church is full of bitty things that people have obviously donated. Bits of carpet, bits of lace cloths on bits of odd furniture, all looking as though they come from the trash and treasure markets. We take photos and try to look interested but can't fake it for long, so go outside, admire the spectacular views out over the sea, and then walk back down again, waving to all the restaurant owners we've passed on the way up, kindly dismissing their offers of meatballs and moussaka, heading for one of the big tourist restaurants lining the beachfront.

We're not even in the mood for lunch, but seeing places full of happy people eating is irresistible to us. We order kebabs from a young waiter with a jar of gel in his thick hair. Next to us is a table full of noisy old plump widows dressed in neck-to-knee black. Greek women whose husbands die before them must wear black for the rest of their lives, unless they marry again. I suppose it makes it easy to buy clothes, and saves decision-making in the morning, but it's not a cheerful look. However, these widows definitely are cheerful. They are of the merry kind. They eat and drink with non-widow-like zest and scream like banshees. What is a banshee anyway? I must find out. One old widow in particular seems to be flirting lustily with the gelled waiter. She appears to be challenging him and he is being politely dismissive.

'There is always something to watch here, isn't there?' I say to Geoffrey.

'Yes, and it would be so much better if only we could understand what they are saying.'

I think it is more fun not knowing what is going on and making up your own scenario. However, in this case I am madly curious, as the widow now scrapes her chair back loudly, waves away the restraining arms of her friends and follows the waiter back inside the restaurant. We can see her at the door.

She makes a big fuss and the owners come out, whereupon one of those typical Greek arguments/conversations/discussions occurs. She finally stamps her feet, adjusts her black head scarf and comes back to sit down with her mates again, still screaming like that banshee I am going to find out about later.

I ask our waiter when he comes to serve us what that was all about. 'Was she flirting with you? Did she proposition you?'

'No,' he says angrily. 'She said she asked for cow's yoghurt, and I gave her sheep's yoghurt. She got angry, and when I told her it was cow's yoghurt and she insisted it wasn't, I asked her did she want donkey's yoghurt—as a joke, because as you very well know, donkeys can't make yoghurt. This made her really angry and she went inside and reported me to the owner.'

So what I thought was flirting was actually serious complaining. And I didn't know you couldn't get yoghurt from a donkey, did you? My thoughts turn to Rebecca for a misty moment, but there is too much going on here for donkey sentiment.

'Are you in trouble with your bosses?' I ask our waiter.

'No, they know me well enough to value me,' he boasts. 'I would leave if they said anything to me. My father is a wealthy man. I don't have to do this kind of work if I don't want to.'

We eat our kebabs, pondering all this while the widows screech and shout on regardless of anyone else in the busy restaurant. On another trip to our table I ask our waiter, son of wealthy parents, where he learnt to speak such perfect English. 'In Australia, of course,' he says. 'That's where my parents first made their money. They owned milk bars and fish and chip shops. Then they came back here and bought lots of land and buildings.'

Of course.

'You see these people,' he says, indicating the loud widows. 'They are not locals. They have come off that tourist bus.' And indeed there are several huge buses out the front of the restaurant, but I never would have picked the black-clad Greek women as tourists.

'They come out for the day from other towns,' our waiter says. 'Old people on tourist buses are worse than children on school buses. When people get old they revert to being like noisy kids. I see it all the time.'

I go very quiet and contemplative at this thought, vowing to make a lady-like descent into old age and never be boisterous on a bus.

'Are you a local then?' I ask as our waiter clears our table.

'Yes, I have lived here all my life apart from my first years; I was born in Australia,' he says, and we then chat about Lesbos and I tell him how much I love Molyvos and how I adored Skala Eressos at the southern end.

'I have never been to Skala Eressos myself,' he says.

I am shocked beyond speech. This local lad has never made the four-hour journey to the bottom of the island. Never been to Skala Eressos. Never seen a lesbian.

'Maybe I will go one day,' he says as though he is contemplating a trip to the other side of the world. With that we pay the bill and give him a big tip because he's been such good entertainment.

And a banshee is a type of ghost, by the way.

We decide to make a day's outing to Eftalou, to the hot mineral springs. Our kind of day, that is, starting at midday. In fact there are many hot springs on Lesbos that have been around since antiquity. They are a reminder of the past volcanic activity in the region, and people come from far to sit in their carbonated, chlorinated, sulphuric, healing waters. If you don't want to pay to go into the baths you can sit just outside them in the sea as all the other tight-fisted people do, where a small current of warm water trickles from the spring.

The springs at Eftalou are as popular as any, and we find them inside a big square stone building. A notice on the wall informs us of the benefits: 'The hot springs of Eftalou are good for chronic rheumatism, arthritis, sciatica, neuralgia, gall stones, gynaecological problems, trauma outcomes, haemorrhoids and dental afflictions.' I suffer from none of these (at least none I am about to reveal to you, although I once had bleeding gums and now I am big on oral hygiene), and also do not fancy immersing myself in near boiling water. Inside the small low room is a little square pool with half a dozen people lying in it—fully costumed, you will be relieved to hear, and is the most claustrophobic space imaginable. Geoffrey decides he wants to go in—for haemorrhoids or his weak bones, he doesn't say—but I opt out. I couldn't bear it.

I go outside and sit on the pebbled beach while he immerses himself. You can obviously only stay in there for a few minutes at a time, because before I can settle into a comfortable spot on the pebbles, Geoffrey comes out, looking and walking like a lobster just out of the boiling pot and throws himself into the cool sea. He repeats this process three more times and finally comes out for good, looking raw and blistered, and saying he's had a terrific time. I strongly doubt it, but he has paid three euros for the pleasure of almost boiling himself alive so he has to pretend. (And Geoffrey doesn't really have haemorrhoids … although he is prone to bunions.)

I try to settle on the pebbles and read my Jackie Collins novel but I'm not enjoying it. Not that I have anything against Jackie Collins novels—they were my lifesavers a couple of decades ago when I was tied down with babies in suburbia. It's just that I can't relate to their flightiness any more. I well remember the time I was so devoted to a Jackie Collins novel that I named one of my daughters after one of her heroines, a lush girl with big boobs and full lips. (Jackie Collins' character, not my daughter, who is now a slim tall girl with perfect boobs and lovely lips.)

We sit for another hour reading, and after Geoffrey has cooled down and his skin has toned down to a nice shade of shocking pink, we go in search of … what else? … food and wine. We climb around the small rocky headland and follow the shore, then spot a little place high up, hanging out over the hill. Up we climb and find a beautiful taverna on the terraced hill. It is spread out over six levels, which must be hard work for the waiters, but the terracing gives it tremendous character. Each level is covered in grapevines and all have views out over the sea. There aren't many customers at this early lunchtime, but those who are here all sit on different levels so the waiter is constantly running up and down.

'Let's see if there is anything different on the menu,' Geoffrey says hopefully. Of course there isn't, and we order Greek salads again, and then a white bean salad because we haven't tried this before. We watch a couple at another table eat slices of canned beetroot on a flat plate with as much appreciation as if it was a plate of truffles. Another couple eat boiled grass, which looks pretty much as though the chef has emptied a bucket of lawn clippings into a pot of boiling water, strained them and put them on a plate. But the locals eat these awful things with real pleasure and much enthusiasm.

'I'd love to take these people back to Australia and show them delicious salads and wonderful food presentation,' I tell Geoffrey. 'I'd love them to experience a salad of rocket with lightly grilled figs, thin layers of prosciutto, scattered with goat's curd, sprinkled with organic walnuts and dressed with a balsamic and olive oil dressing. Wouldn't you?'

'Be quiet and eat your canned white beans,' he says, so I do. The house wine is acceptable every place we go and the Mythos beer that Geoffrey drinks is outstanding, according to him. So who cares about canned beans and beetroot and boiled grass?

We are enjoying the peace of the quiet restaurant, idly watching the entertainment provided by the waiter puffing up and down the levels, when in comes the biggest group booking we have ever seen. Dozens and dozens of attractive young people flood in at once, taking up every table, every bit of space in the restaurant. They rearrange tables, pull out chairs, add tables to more tables, sit down, get up, move tables, sit down again, scrape chairs and call out loudly to each other from all levels of the restaurant. They all have big bags, bikini tops and bare torsos. Several of them are babes. Lots of them are hunks. One of them looks like the deranged cousin you let out of the attic for special occasions. I have one of the hunks backed right on to me. His chair bangs against mine and I curse under my breath until he turns to me says in sexy accented English, 'Is it okay?'

'Of course it is, no trouble at all; you aren't bothering me in the least.' I can be hypocritical, as well as shallow and bitchy sometimes.

We spend a happy hour eavesdropping on their conversations. We cannot understand a word, but love the way they shout over each other, reach across the table to spear the last forkful of calamari, dip their bread in the Greek salad oil, smoke all over each other, and generally make a hell of a happy noise.

I am seething with curiosity as to who they are.

'Ask them,' Geoffrey says. I don't want to, but it does give me an excuse to tap on the big beautiful bare shoulder of the hunk behind me.

'Are you a family group?' I manage when he turns and fixes me with chocolate drop eyes and George Michael stubble.

'No, we are all artists,' he says, very friendly. 'We are from the Athens School of Fine Art.'

'You are on a study tour?'

'Sort of. We go to look at museums and monasteries (the way he says 'monasteries' makes it sound like 'you are a fine specimen of lush womanhood') and paintings and sculptures.'

We then get into an interesting conversation, as though we have been friends all our lives. I love the friendliness of the Greeks and their willingness to talk to big fat strangers in restaurants. He talks about Lesbos, other Greek islands he loves, and then about Athens. I comment that Athens is a little torn up at the moment with all the building for the Olympics going on.

He nods his head sadly.

'We are so tired of it all,' he says. 'It has been a nightmare for so long. And Greeks are not fast workers. I don't know if it will be ready in time. Greeks are very slow, very slow. We have too many of the day offs too. But we have a way of making it all happen at the end, very quickly.'

'I know you will.' I say sympathetically because sometimes I can be nice as well as hypocritical and shallow and bitchy.

'You should come to Australia,' I invite. I say this to everyone I meet on holiday, knowing they will give me that wistful look and say, 'Yes, I'd love to, I'd love to, but it's too far.'

'I'd love to, I'd love to, but it's too far,' he sighs. 'But there is one place I know about in Australia, and that is Philip Island. That place alone would make me get on a plane for long hours.'

Good lord. Philip Island? Yes, the motorbike racing. He watches it on television and has fallen madly in love with Philip Island.

We part the best of friends; I promise to send him some information on Philip Island.

You can keep your bouzouki halls, your Greek dancing and your plate smashing. You can even keep your concerts in magical castle settings. There is theatre enough all around you in Greece, in every taverna and café all over the land. And it's free.

A SMALL DETOUR
TO MALTA

Well, here we are in Malta. I apologise for yanking you out of Greece without warning, but the unexpected can often happen when you're doing a long trip and have allowed yourself to be flexible. Let me explain. An email came from an Australian business acquaintance now living in Belgium.

'I'm getting married in Malta next week,' she said. 'If you're in Europe, we'd love you to join us.' We thought about it for a full ten minutes, then jumped on a couple of planes and here we are.

'If we lived in Europe, we could do this sort of thing all the time,' I tell Geoffrey, because living in Europe for its summer months every year is part of my long-term plan as I move further and faster into old-ladyhood.

Malta is a place you rarely think about. Be honest, when was the last time you gave Malta a thought? For me it was more than three decades ago, when I met an English couple who moved there to escape paying high UK taxes; they paid just sixpence tax in every English pound there. They used to brag about it and make us envious—we were living in England at the time and paying about half of every pound in tax. But then house prices or the general economy plunged in Malta, I forget which, probably both, and suddenly their lifestyle was devalued and they returned to England, disillusioned and generally pretty pissed off.

Most of us know Malta sits somewhere low in the Mediterranean, even though we aren't sure where, and we know it's a small rocky island, but that's about it. Actually, one other thing Geoffrey and I know about Malta is that Brad Pitt is here at the moment, filming *Troy*. A potential Brad Pitt sighting plus a wedding was more than enough enticement for us to change plans and hot-foot it over here.

We're staying in the swish Westins Dragonara Resort, which is set on its own peninsula, if you don't mind, in the area of St Julian's. Our room looks out to sea, and to the resort's lavish pool area and the Bedouin Bar, which stretches to the water's edge, where the wedding ceremony will take place tomorrow.

Malta is small—smaller than the Isle of Wight, the person at hotel reception told us when he'd regained his composure after doing that little jumping back thing when we approached him. Malta has a fascinating history. It has suffered thousands of years of invasions, from the Phoenicians, Arabs and Romans to the most documented, the Knights of the Order of St John, and an attempt during World War II by the Germans. Why so many people would want to invade such a small and rocky island requires you to wonder—Malta doesn't have gold or copper riches or endless oil supplies or even flourishing olive groves, but when you consider Malta's marvellous strategic position in the Mediterranean, it is easy to see why. Every captain of every ship sailing by for the past several thousand years—and there must have been millions on this busy route—must have thought, 'What a spiffing little stop-off place. I can see a good use for it for my own country', and sailed happily in to shore to fight battles and take over for a short while, until another captain on another ship sailed merrily by and thought the same thing.

Rich in history Malta may be, but sadly, nothing about it has impressed us so far. The drive from the airport revealed pot-holed roads, neglected fields of long brown grass, cracked and broken foot-paths, abandoned shops, empty workshops, overflowing rubbish bins, and in general gave us the impression that Malta is a place where the people don't have much national pride. However, the Dragonara Resort is an oasis of glamour and jet-setting gorgeousness. The wedding celebrations include not only a reception in a secret location tomorrow, but also a cruise out to the Blue Lagoon—this is where the movie of the same name was filmed, and where Brad Pitt is filming right now.

We cruised yesterday, and I have to say that Malta is far more beautiful from the sea than it is on shore. We sailed around the island in a big wooden junk-type ship (I really must make an effort to find out the proper names for these things), past tall chalky cliffs rising dramatically from the sea and around the more appealing (so we are told) island of Gozo, then anchored in the vivid blue water of the lagoon. On the nearby shore we could see the *Troy* filming. Helicopters—presumably with aerial cameras—flew overhead and we all strained our necks and eyes on the decks for a Brad Pitt sighting, but we were just too far away.

Most people in the wedding party are from Belgium but there is an interesting couple of gay women from London. As Geoffrey and I are honorary lesbians, we warmed to Annie and Anya immediately and we spent so long chatting on the sunny deck, and lunching on salads and roast beef and bread, that we all got sunburnt. But we bonded, and I think Annie and Anya were tremendously jealous of our holiday in Lesbos.

Like the Greeks, a lot of Maltese have lived in Australia and then returned to their home country to retire. The 20-something chef in charge of catering on the boat said he spent most of his childhood in

Australia before his parents brought him back to Malta. He was keen to talk to us.

'I loved Australia, but Malta is great too,' he said. 'You need to stay a month on Malta for me to show you around properly,' he continued, which we thought was pretty generous for someone whose acquaintance we had just made when he handed us a roast beef sandwich. But stay in Malta a month? We didn't like it enough to stay a week. Judgemental and shallow … I told you.

'There is so much to see here in Malta, it would actually take about two months, and still you wouldn't have seen everything,' the chef said, but then, 'and I would show you it all if I wasn't so busy. Another sandwich?'

After the cruise, we showered and went out to explore the area of St Julian's, outside the Dragonara Resort. But as soon as we left the ordered neatness of the resort we were in another world: we tripped over cracked concrete on footpaths so narrow it was impossible for two people to walk side by side; a woman holding a cigarette accidentally burnt my arm as she tried to squeeze past me. There were a few small, depressing shops selling postcards and junky beach equipment, and one or two modern restaurants, but they sat beside derelict buildings with smashed beer bottles lying in doorways and mangy cats prowling over bursting garbage bags. We had a meal of very good spaghetti in an almost empty grungy Italian restaurant and went back to the Dragonara feeling disheartened.

This morning, after I manage to set off the smoke alarms in the hotel dining room while using the toaster at the breakfast buffet, we make plans to get out and explore while the bride spends the day in the beauty salon. We talk to ourselves harshly. 'Keep an open mind; don't judge; go forth and explore Malta, enjoy.'

After queuing for forty frustrating minutes in the local bank to change money, our optimism and high spirits have completely gone, but we board a ratty bus for the historic town of Valletta. This bus looks like the ones I remember from my childhood in the 1950s, and later someone tells us the Maltese buses were all indeed built in the 1950s, and still operating. But it costs about 20 cents to go from one part of the island to another so we put up with the torn seats, pull down the filthy windows to let in a bit of breeze and stare out at broken concrete, run-down houses, and piles of rubble in front gardens. We do not see a cheerful windowbox or a flower-filled terracotta tub anywhere.

But what the scenery lacks, the Maltese people make up for. They are very friendly, speak English, and are fascinated by Australia. Our taxi driver yesterday told us the Maltese language is a mix of Arabic, Spanish, Greek, Italian plus a few dozen others that I can't remember now. Clearly, if so many people had invaded your country over the last two thousand years, myriad influences would affect every aspect of society, from the language to the food and architecture; this obviously is what makes Malta so fascinating. If only it could fascinate us.

Malta has no natural resources, so its history and guaranteed summer sunshine are its main attractions, and the new and elaborate hotel and apartment buildings around the harbour and the impressive newly constructed walkways are a sign that the Maltese are serious about attracting visitors. But for now, the new places and the smart harbour-side walkway clash with the general air of neglect.

Our bus drops us off in the square outside the old city walls of Valletta—a town built in the sixteenth century by the Knights of St John—and this certainly lifts our mood. An enormous and elaborate fountain dominates the square, but the square also acts as the bus terminal, and those 1950s rattlers don't quite go with the grandness of the fountain. We walk through the city gates into the wide, long and imposing Republic Street, and at last get a feeling for just how marvellous Malta really is. Shops, museums, churches and stately buildings line the street, and on this sunny Saturday morning hundreds of people walking around create a colourful flowing river down its width. We wander to the end, stopping for a while at Republic Square, in front of the impressive National Library. We refuse the many offers of a horse and carriage ride and take to the side streets looking for *The Malta Experience*, a cinematic show we have been told is amazing—it will not only enthral us but give us a good idea of Malta's 7000 years of history.

'Once you've seen *The Malta Experience* you will have a true feel for Malta,' the chef on the boat told us yesterday. 'Then you will want to come with me around the island for a month to see everything, and we could do it to if I had the time, but I don't.'

The Malta Experience is a slide show, but with a dramatic narration and rousing music, and it is fascinating and informative, and goes a long way to explain why the Maltese now don't bother planting flowers in terracotta pots. For the last 7000 years, just as they had their houses and gardens in order, invaders barged in, messed it all up and took over. The great siege of Malta in 1565 was one of the bloodiest attempts to fight off an invasion. Locals had their heads cut off and their bodies nailed to wooden planks and floated down the river. The enemy—the Portuguese at that time if my memory is right, but it could have been anyone from a dozen or more other countries—retaliated by cutting off the heads of prisoners and shooting them out of cannons.

'That was thoroughly enjoyable,' I comment to Geoffrey as we leave, and then almost burst into tears as two of the horse carriage men get into a fight over a potential customer.

We catch another appalling bus to Mdina, the historic walled town. Quietness is the rule here; the only form of transport allowed is horse-drawn carriage. Even talking loudly is forbidden. Our friend the chef told us we would be physically removed from the lovely old town if we yelled. As we are occasionally wont to do this to each other, we prepare ourselves mentally to be calm before we get off the bus and walk through the stone gates into the town. It is a bit like what I imagine entering the Holy Land would feel like: so quiet, so reverent. As in a church, speaking seems out of order in here.

A tiny woman dressed in a costume of ancient times stands on a corner; she looks as though she has stepped out of the pages of a child's book. As we approach, she thrusts a brochure at us, urging us to see *The Mdina Experience*, a cinematic show—subtitled *Tales of the Silent City*—depicting thousands of years of the history of Mdina. 'Feel the earth shake', the leaflet promises. 'Travel through three thousand years of Mdina's history; the Arab domination, the Norman period, the Great Siege and late baroque, the French and British rule, and more.' The poor Maltese people. They haven't had a moment's peace for thousands of years. We're tempted for a few minutes, but the thought of watching more invasions exhausts us. We wander on, much to the tiny woman's disappointment as there aren't many tourists here at this time.

We stop to look at the ornate buildings lining the paved streets and we linger in St Paul's Square by the magnificent church with two bell towers, one on each side, with clocks underneath the ornate carving.

The narrow streets flanked by tall buildings branch off into a confusing maze. It was obviously built this way so that the locals could run around the labyrinth and escape yet another lot of invading rotters. It's very peaceful in here now, and the old buildings with overhanging balconies could no doubt tell us a thing or two about the town's history, but there are no lively little cafés or shops or restaurants where you can stop, sit and reflect. It is very romantic at night, apparently, with old-fashioned street lamps the only form of lighting. We would like to stay until darkness but we have a wedding to attend, so we content ourselves with a 'Mdina in the Afternoon' experience and then take the bus back to St Julian's. It is the worst bus in the world, and we spend the whole trip sitting on ripped seats with bits of yellow foam sticking to our legs, looking apprehensively at the greasy bucket of mechanic's tools beside the driver's shabby seat.

We assemble at the Bedouin Bar on the water's edge of the hotel and wait for the beautiful bride to arrive, bonding a little more with Annie and Anya, who we now find out are actually legally married.

The bride enters in a designer dress of breathtaking gorgeousness, and after the ceremony the Moët champagne corks pop. We then take a line of cars to our secret location, which turns out to be the Maltese Yacht Club. Now by Australian standards that doesn't sound like a swish venue, but let me tell you, the Maltese Yacht Club resembles an ancient castle and overlooks the river, looking across to the fortress walls of Valletta. It is one hell of a romantic spot, and at this time of evening, with the fierce sun fading, the fortress walls are almost pink. We drink more Moët and eat oysters and suckling pig cooked by our chef from the boat yesterday ('Hi, have some pig, it's delicious, and I'd love to show you around Malta for the next four weeks if only I didn't have to work') and dance in the incredible setting, stopping every ten minutes to gaze out to the fortress walls and say, 'Hooley dooley, is this fabulous?'

After the recovery brunch the next morning the bride and groom leave for a St Tropez honeymoon and we sit by the pool reading the local papers with Annie and Anya—but not before we make plans with the hotel's helpful concierge to get us the hell out of Malta this evening. We are so close to Sicily we've decided to make a stopover there before going back to Greece.

If reading English newspapers thrills me, I can't tell you what excitement I get from reading newspapers in countries I know nothing about. Reading about politicians, personalities and identities I have never heard of or could care less about, but who feature so largely in the lives of others, is especially satisfying. According to today's Maltese headline, almost 70 per cent of the people are happy with the government's direction (the Nationalist Party is in power) and 81.3 per cent want the Maltese Labour Party to embrace EU membership. Malta is on the verge of joining. The Prime Minister, Dr Fenech Adami, is going to step down and a Dr Lawrence Gonzi is the likely new PM— and I'm glad I've told you all that, even though I have a strong suspicion you could not give a toss who governs Malta.

This newspaper has an abundance of columnists who write prodigiously in flowery text. One wrote almost an entire page about how we should be supporting a local lass called Lynn Chircop, who wants to participate in the Eurovision Song Contest in her own way, not according to the rules, and is being vilified by the Maltese population for ruining their hopes in the contest.

'Everyone is entitled to moments of relaxation and light entertainment, from whichever source this may come,' the columnist writes. 'To make such moments a national issue is ridiculous. Either we are ready to participate, do our best, and then enjoy the show, or else we have to take tranquillisers to keep our heads level.' Make of that what you will.

It gets better on page ten. Here we have the exciting news that Elton John is coming to Malta to perform a one-off concert. However, we are told not to watch out for Elton, à la Brad Pitt, walking down the street, because he's flying in on his private jet just before the concert (and slightly after his piano) and will fly straight out the minute he finishes. He must feel the same way as we do about Malta.

Anya and Annie invite us to their home in London next week for a quick visit and we are tempted. They appear very excited, urge us to think about it, and even write up a busy itinerary for the visit.

'You must come,' they encourage. 'We even have good plumbing in our apartment.'

'Pardon?'

'You know the English are not renowned for their good plumbing. We can all shower together at our place.'

'Excuse me?'

'I mean at once. You know, when someone is in one shower it doesn't matter if someone in the other bathroom is showering at the same time. Our plumbing is very good.'

As tempted as we are by the good English plumbing, we doubt we can do it. Our plan is to spend this summer in Greece, and here we are in Malta, about to set off for Sicily.

Later, as we wait with our luggage for a taxi outside the hotel, our friend the chef wanders by.

'You're leaving?' he says, astonished. 'But I thought you were going to stay a month, there is so much to do. And I was going to show you around, if only I had the time.'

ANOTHER DETOUR
TO SICILY

We love Sicily, but not at first sight, because we arrive at one in the morning and have an hour and a half drive along the boring motorway from the airport in Catania to Taormina, the place we have been told is the most beautiful spot on the island. But it is definitely love at second sight from the tall windows in our room on the third floor of the gracious, grand and grossly expensive Excelsior Hotel.

Our driver, a man with fluent English, thanks to an English mother, entertained us all the way from the airport with information about Sicily—mostly to do with the refugee problem and the whims of the local people—and even came into the Excelsior's reception with us at three in the morning to assist with check-in, which was just as well, because the sleepy old man behind the counter came wide awake and startled with one quick look at us. But our driver took control.

'La camera, bella vista?' he inquired sternly of the man behind the desk. My Italian was good enough to know the inquiry was about the beauty of the view from our room—and it had better be good.

'*Si, si,*' the receptionist said. '*Molto bella vista.*'

In the morning when we wake and throw back the heavy gold curtains on the narrow windows, the vista is so very *bella*, I shout '*bella vista*', '*bella vista*' back to Geoffrey, who is still snoring on the bed, and then keep saying it over and over for the next twenty-four hours because I can occasionally be boring and annoying as well as judgmental and shallow.

The hotel concierge in Malta had made this booking at the Excelsior for us, and he'd warned us that the hotel would be expensive. One look out our window this morning and we can see why. Our bella vista takes in the hotel's groomed subtropical gardens, a long sparkling pool perched on the ledge of a cliff over a shimmering ocean to the imposing green mountains beyond. We like this very much, and immediately look at our guidebook. Taormina is a small town on the northeastern side of the island, famous for its marvellous position above the sea on a spur of Mt Tauro. The town has an intriguing history, beautiful beaches, renowned restaurants, glamorous shops, sassy nightlife, an ancient Greek theatre and stunning views of the magnificent Mt Etna, one of the world's most active volcanoes.

'This place is definitely me, me, me,' I shout to Geoffrey, who looks deeply worried, because he knows this means I want to stay here a good while and one night at the Excelsior has already cost us the equivalent of a year's mortgage payments back home.

'We'll have to see if we can find somewhere cheaper if we're going to stay,' he says. I am in the mood to compromise because one thing is certain, there are hundreds of charming hotels in this place and there must be something less expensive.

After we've breakfasted in the grand dining room on watery orange juice and hard bread and jam, we go out and find such a place, the Villa Schuler: boutique, refurbished, sitting on a hill, magnificent views. As we approach the reception counter with our large suitcases and even larger smiles the male receptionist does the biggest double take we have experienced so far. He looks terrified of us.

'What do you want?' he says. 'A garage?'

A garage?

'We want a room,' we tell him politely, which seems only to confuse him further, but after more frightened looks and a couple of startled leaps back from the counter as we lean over, he reluctantly delves into his reservation book, shakes his head, steps even further back and finally tells us he can let us have a room for five days.

'Why do people look at us as though we've walked in with two heads each or big hunchbacks or something?' I ask Geoffrey as he unpacks in our room, which looks out over lush gardens to one side and Mt Etna to the other. 'And what the hell would he think we want a garage for?'

'He must rent garages,' Geoffrey says. 'These narrow streets are one way and very tight, hadn't you noticed? Parking would be at a premium. Perhaps he thought we had a car we wanted to put somewhere.'

We'll never know, because I do not want to have to talk to him again unless it's absolutely necessary. The way these hotel people react to us is starting to bother me.

Taormina is located on a plateau below Mt Tauro and is 200 metres above sea level. That means beautiful big views out over sparkling sea, which in turn means charm and allure, which in another turn means Taormina must be an internationally known hot spot for wealthy holiday-makers, which in a further turn means big prices for everything. We had not heard of it until yesterday (we really do have to get out more), but now read and discover. It appears famous people have been holidaying in Taormina for years. It became very fashionable in the 1920s among celebrities and the wealthy, and even more fashionable in the 1950s, when it became known as a 'bathing resort', and also for its film festival. Ava Gardner and her friends used to kick up their heels at La Giara, the pretty restaurant on the terrace above us which we can see from our garden window.

'Wow, Ava Gardner used to go to that restaurant,' I tell Geoffrey and point out the window.

'Oh, was she there last night?' he says. He really does need to get out more, a lot more even than me. The list of famous people who have enjoyed Taormina seems endless. Liz Taylor and Richard Burton were regular visitors. D.H. Lawrence lived here from 1920 to 1930. Truman Capote wrote *Breakfast at Tiffany's* and *In Cold Blood* here. Cecil Beaton, Jean Cocteau, Osbert Sitwell, Salvador Dali, Orson Welles, John Steinbeck, Tennessee Williams, Rita Hayworth, Greta Garbo and Cary Grant have all stayed here. Countless famous writers have lived and worked in Taormina over the years, no doubt scratching out masterpieces with old inky pens. I feel like such a writer myself right now as I set up my laptop just inside the French doors which look out to a small balcony and over to Mt Etna.

'I could stay here for forever looking up from my keyboard to this view, writing like Tennessee Williams,' I mention to Geoffrey, who is now sunbathing on the balcony, but the romance is kind of spoilt by my big knickers hanging out to dry on a bit of string along the balcony, not to mention Geoffrey sprawled plumply next to them in nothing but his brief black underpants.

In the morning we eat breakfast on the sunny terrace—eggs, bread, croissants, juice and coffee—and look down to the sea and across to Mt Etna. We decide that returning to Greece can wait awhile. Even Geoffrey has settled into dreaminess; he hasn't mentioned the horrendous cost of this place for two peaceful minutes. We continue reading from the guidebook and think back to some of the information our driver had given us.

'Sicilians love to come out and walk in Taormina,' he had told us the other night. 'They just walk up and down, showing off their new mobile phone, their new jacket, their new anything. It is a pastime the locals would not live without.' We were passing a large boarded construction site at the time and our informative driver also told us it was supposed to be a new and much needed car park but work had been halted on the project because Roman ruins had been found as soon as they started to dig.

'This is a common occurrence whenever developers build anything,' he said. 'The island is riddled with ruins and it is so normal to stumble upon them that workers will keep quiet about it and not inform authorities because it means a halt on the work.'

Unbelievable.

We venture out to explore, taking the stone steps overlooking the luxuriant gardens up from the Villa Schuler to the Corso Umberto, the main pedestrian-only street, which is lined with glamorous shops and enticing restaurants—and those poor African men selling wooden toys and bits of junk on blankets on the ground. The Corso is punctuated by several delightful squares and lined with beautiful fifteenth-century palazzos, which are now *patisseries* and *gelaterias*, and at each end it has a medieval gate, the Porta Messina and the Porta Catania, which give us a little thrill just to walk through.

Even more fascinating to me than the designer shops full of Armani, Prada and Gucci labels are the little shops selling colourful marzipan delicacies shaped into perfect miniature fruits and vegetables. Pears, peaches, zucchini, eggplants, apples, artichokes, watermelons and bananas look far too beautiful to eat—I can't believe anyone could bite into such exquisiteness—and are so appealing we take a dozen photos of them, probably to the annoyance of the shopkeepers, because we don't buy any.

In the morning we walk for hours in the sunshine, exploring small stepped side streets, sitting over coffees in the piazzas, looking down from various vantage points to the Mediterranean below, so flat and calm the boats and lavish yachts look as though they are not moving, like toys that could fit in your hand. We walk up to the Greek Theatre and debate whether to pay 4.5 euros each to go inside—we are often so stingy it astounds even us—and decide that if we are here we may as well wander around the remains of this ancient theatre. The minute we step inside our mouths gape and we go silent. A mere 4.5 euros to be inside this stupendous place, to sit high up in the theatre on one of the stone seats of the rows that curve around the stage, looking down to the columns of the stage area and over to the view—we could have paid 40 euros and still it wouldn't have been too much.

The Greek Theatre has a remarkable position: it's high on a hill, and offers one of the most breathtaking views to Mt Etna in all Sicily. This view has been painted thousands of times and described by countless writers. 'Never did any audience, in any theatre, have before it such a spectacle,' Goethe said in 1787; this pretty much sums up my feelings. We stay in the theatre for a long time, sitting on the concrete steps at the very top, watching workmen erecting tall black screens on the stage between the soaring columns, fussing with wires and installing lighting. The thought of sitting high up in here at night when the theatre is full of people and the ancient columns and walls are lit up makes me come out in goose bumps.

We think of Ida and her amphitheatre back in Noosa and wish she was here to talk to us, to instil in us that special feeling for history that comes so easily to her—and so that this place could get into her soul as it has into ours. We remember back to one of her amphitheatre concerts in Noosa, when distant rain threatened and the entertainers refused to perform in case the rain fell on their electrical equipment and electrocuted them. (Fair enough, I suppose.) Ida was sick with nerves, because hundreds of people were sitting in her amphitheatre, expecting a magical evening concert. All around the amphitheatre people were popping champagne corks and delving into picnic baskets for pâtés and cheeses, and hovering over the open-air theatre in the damp air was the unmistakable feeling of anticipation. Behind the scenes Ida was pleading with the entertainers to risk electrocution and perform. So convincing is this little woman that they actually did and it turned out to be a memorable night of music in a spectacular setting. And no-one died, you'll be pleased to hear.

Much later we wander back down to the entrance of the Greek Theatre and inquire of a bald man at the ticket box what the erecting of the screens is for, what type of entertainment is about to held here.

'The famous film festival,' he says happily. 'But not until next week. Perhaps after you have left?' His face lights up.

We compensate by having lunch beneath a canopy of lemon trees and grapevines in the delightful outdoor section of a restaurant called La Botte. A black-clad mamma and stern papa sit at a table just near the door counting money, watching their staff—their sons and daughters, no doubt—serving the customers spaghetti, gnocchi, pizzas and carafes of bright yellow wine.

Alessandro—his name is printed in huge letters on the back of his shirt—brings us a pizza with black olives and anchovies, and spaghetti with tomato sauce and parmesan, and so much wine we go back to the Villa Schuler and snore the afternoon away.

It is nine o'clock in the evening before we venture out again. It's light still, although fading, and we walk along the Corso Umberto once more, this time being swept along a current of people at *passeggiata*, that strolling thing the Italians love to do.

'Boy, they love the *passeggiata* here,' I mention to Geoffrey as we try to get around groups of five, six, sometimes eight people all strolling abreast with arms linked, taking up the entire width of the Corso.

'Why don't we do this walking up and down thing so much back home?' I wonder out loud. 'It is so delightful so see friends, lovers, families all out together in their good clothes just walking and enjoying the evening.'

We join couples holding hands, parents with wide-awake children, young attractive people and old handsome people, all strolling happily. But Geoffrey and I find it difficult to walk slowly. We are the brisk walking types and we manoeuvre around the wide groups several times before becoming exasperated and taking to the side streets. We stroll until we are hungry but then can't choose a restaurant from the abundance of choices all around us. We promise to stop at the very next one, and this happens to be the Ristorante Pizzeria Taormina, down yet another small side street but with attractive views from the terrace over geranium-filled terracotta pots to the streets below.

A handsome middle-aged American couple at the table next to us sit very still and serious. She has a dish of something in front of her that looks like a giant seashell. It is taking up most of her plate, towering impressively high, looking like something that has been washed up on a beach on a tropical island. I guess it is calamari, but it is clear that whatever it is, this woman is not about to touch it. We order spaghetti with chilli and tagliatelle with a mushroom sauce, and then swordfish and chicken, and then complain about how much weight we're gaining. I try to concentrate on my food but I can't take my eyes off the woman's untouched dinner. At last the friendly waiter comes over to see what is wrong with her dish, and sure enough, she tells him she thought that when she ordered calamari she would get tiny strips, not this big sea monster sitting in front of her. He explains that that's the way calamari is prepared here; she is horrified, so he says he will bring her something else. She demurs but he insists, and brings her prawns, which she nibbles on with great trepidation. It makes me laugh.

I love Americans, they are among my favourite people in the world, but they do so expect to find everything similar to things in their own country when they travel. The waiter is most perplexed now and keeps coming over to the Americans to ask if everything is okay. Then he becomes anxious about us—unnecessarily, because the gluttonous Rickards can eat anything, even if it does look as if it has just leapt out of the sea onto our plates. I try to reassure him by saying our food is *molto bella*, but he corrects me, saying that *bella* means beautiful; *buono* is the more appropriate form of address for food. '*Bella* applies to a woman,' he says, looking at me with slitted eyes, as though I have just called his food sexually thrilling. Or perhaps he was thinking *bella* was a word more appropriate to me.

When we leave the restaurant at 11.30 pm the streets are still packed with people of all ages at *passeggiata*.

'Look at these young kids and babies still wide awake,' I comment, frustrated for a moment by the way the street is clogged by the strolling people. But then I sigh with contentment, link arms with darling Geoffrey and stroll slowly and happily back to the hotel, smiling benignly (stupidly, actually) at everyone coming in my direction.

CLIMBING MT ETNA

We have looked at the view of Mt Etna for too long. It's time to get close to it, to go up it. Tour buses galore go up there each day and we make a booking. We are not good at tours, do not like being with groups or in big crowds. If someone out there knows what it is about a tour that makes everyone anxious to be the first person on the bus, I'd appreciate it if they could tell me. The small crowd waiting to board this morning surges forward as one urgent mass when the bus pulls in to the depot. We crush around the narrow door, preventing the tour leader, who is already on the empty bus, from getting off. It's only when he squeezes through the throng and speaks sternly to us that we realise we are at the wrong bus. We melt away sheepishly—we were acting like sheep, so sheepishly really is the right word—and wait quietly, only to surge again as the correct bus finally arrives.

Once we've all surged to our full surging extent and are sitting in our seats glaring at each other, the tour leader introduces herself on the microphone in four languages. Everything she says—and there is much to say on the hour drive up the mountain—is repeated in English,

German, French and Sicilian. However, as annoying as this is, there is an Italian woman with a mannish voice two seats behind us who is the clear winner in the annoying stakes. She is talking loudly on her mobile phone to someone called Franco, who appears to have locked himself in the *bagno,* the bathroom, the toilet. She seems to be giving Franco loud and detailed instructions on how to get himself out of the *bagno.* An English woman directly behind us—from Cornwall, judging by her strong accent—finally tells Franco Woman to shut up and we continue listening to the tour leader in four languages until Franco Woman gets loudly back on the mobile phone with *bagno* instructions again. This goes on until we reach the top of Mt Etna and has so irritated us that we have not enjoyed the breathtaking views or the scenic villages on the way up. When we get out of the bus we see that Franco Woman is 40-something and wearing a neck brace. (Had someone tried to shove her head through a door recently?) She's on the phone again, pacing up and down the car park, yelling frantically and waving her arms in the air. This woman appears on bus tours all around the world. I'm sure you've encountered her. She is the one who drops her heavy hand luggage on your head as she struggles with the overhead compartment; the one who usually sits in front of you and puts her seat back so far her head is in your lap; the one who is always, always, so late back for the bus that a search party has to go looking for her while everyone on the bus seethes with anger.

We are at the base camp of Mt Etna, as far up as the road and buses can go. We must now prepare ourselves to trek around the spectacular mountain with another guide. Geoffrey and I are, of course, the only people without jackets and boots. In the heat of the Taormina morning when we left we had not given thought to the fact that being high up on a mountain might just mean a bit of chill in the air. We shiver, hug our arms to our chests and generally look stupid while everyone else digs into backpacks for warm jackets and sturdy shoes. Fortunately, there is a shop nearby for idiots to hire such things, and we struggle into jackets too small and I try to squeeze into boots too tight because there is no way I am about to tell our hot young guide that my feet are at least two sizes bigger than the size 41s he's offering me. We also hire impressive hiking sticks—we may be uncomfortable, but we sure look the part of volcano trekkers.

Mt Etna is the highest volcano in Europe and one of the largest and most active in the world. Fortunately it is at rest now, but a couple of years ago it was in full fiery flight, no doubt giving the locals pause for thought. We are told that the locals actually live surprisingly easily with the constant threat of boiling lava flowing down on them. They accept that Mt Etna might bring the occasional hot sparks, cascading boulders and rivers of molten rock, because it also brings tourists and money and happy activity to their otherwise quiet and poor villages. Mt Etna is nearly 40 kilometres in diameter at the base. Now that's big. From the distance, as we have seen it so often these past days, it appears almost perfectly regular in shape, and because it is so wide, it doesn't look very high. But it is 3500 metres tall and it has four open summit craters and 300 side craters rising from a truncated cone. I am remembering all this with difficulty, because as I said, our guide is a hot young stud and he has a sexy accent so it is impossible to concentrate fully on what he's saying, especially with the backdrop of the brilliant black lava fields.

We begin our trek, walking in a long line. The ground around us is so vast and starkly black we could be on another planet. While the scene might not be quite on the scale of the Grand Canyon as far as sheer astonishment goes, it is almost as astounding looking out to these great peaks and cosmic valleys of bright blackness. High up in the distance we can see the tiny figures of another tour group walking single file along a massive dark crater edge. It looks like a surreal scene from a science fiction movie.

The hard lava is crunchy beneath our boots but it does not stick or leave a black mark. Our hiking sticks prove to be a real benefit; far more than just vain accessories as we poke them into the black surface and pull ourselves on and up. It is thrilling just being here, despite

Franco Woman, now behind us and still yelling, although not on the phone but to other people in the group now. We stop by small clumps of green bushes and yellow wildflowers growing healthily out of the black stones, and our guide picks flowers, passes them around and tells us what they are—I now can't remember what he said because I was looking at his buttocks, beautifully outlined in his jeans, as he bent over. He tells us that when Etna was exploding in 2001 he stayed up near the hot lava for as long as he could to take pictures, and this little tale of bravery adds to his already abundant sex appeal. He also tells us that taking people on Mt Etna tours is his summer job; in the winter he is a ski instructor. My lust swells.

We climb higher and I lag back to take photos of the group against the starkness of the landscape. In the still air their voices travel sweetly back to me (apart from Franco Woman's) and it is all very dreamlike.

'The lava it goes 100 metres, 1000 metres, 100 metres,' our sexy guide says. At least that's what I thought he said, because his accent, while fabulous, makes understanding difficult. 'When the lava goes into a little cave, remains there a lot of gas,' he says. 'When the gas go up in the form of the little cave, little oven, it makes big noise.' He makes a gesture to demonstrate the gas going up the little oven, by putting his finger through a hole made by circling his thumb and forefinger. I go wobbly at the knees.

We pass enormous craters, climb high peaks, and look out across black valleys, and finally we come to a huge abyss. I ask our guide if anyone has ever fallen into one of these deep crevices, and if they did, how would they get out: helicopters, ropes, a huge rescue effort? But he doesn't understand my question: he thinks I've asked if anyone has ever been killed up here.

'One photographer, he get his legs cut off when he get too close to a crater and a huge boulder came flying down and whip the legs off.'

That shuts us all up for a while, except Franco Woman.

We hike on to a narrow but frighteningly deep hole, fenced off with a flimsy bit of tape. It is 25 metres deep and we all take turns stepping up cautiously to its edge to peer nervously down. At this point we are all tempted to give Franco Woman a gentle nudge with our hiking sticks, and one or two of us even aim them at her as she bends over the hole. We peer until we have peered enough, as you do when you are a group peering, and then we walk on to a particularly steep slope, where we skid helplessly down before digging our heels into the soft black dirt to stop ourselves tumbling forward. As we gather momentum everyone shrieks and squeals, and we finally all fall into a tumble at the bottom, laughing at the exhilarating experience.

It would be very easy to get lost up here, as all the valleys and peaks lead to yet more valleys and peaks, and the moon-like landscape is very confusing. It is just as well Geoffrey and I decided not to be stingy and pay the extra 12 euros each for the guide rather than go by ourselves. Finally, we pass big boulders giving out heat like radiators, and our guide stops to put a piece of newspaper against one of them. It immediately browns and catches alight and we all make appropriate impressed noises. Even Franco Woman appears impressed.

'Here are the 50 metres of the lava in 2001,' our guide says. I'll leave it up to you to make out what that means; I'm only repeating it because it sounds so sexy on my tape recorder. He then tells us how beautiful it is up here in the first snows of winter, because the white snow against the back mountain is quite incredible, and we can well imagine the glorious scene.

After an hour and a half of trekking and feeling like mountaineers, we finally arrive back at the point where we began, and I say a sad goodbye to our gorgeous guide and wonder—just for a ridiculous old-woman moment—if I might get away with a mouth kiss instead of a handshake. I don't try it, of course. We pass by huge campervans full of people in the car park. They have the doors open and most are sitting inside drinking cups of tea or coffee or soup and eating their own sandwiches. For a moment I feel quite offended that they are not contributing a cent to the tourism industry of this place but that is just my inner bitch talking. They probably paid for the car park and bought their bread and ingredients locally. And besides, I have conveniently just forgotten that I've told you how I hate spending money myself.

We have been told to meet for lunch in a lodge-like restaurant at the base camp, and we all scramble to be the first in to get a seat. Don't scoff, this tour group mentality of having to be the first to eat, drink, get on the bus or in line is hard to resist. Franco Woman catches the eye of the harried waiter first and places a complicated order which takes up a good ten minutes of his time. Everyone else fumes and huffs.

After a lunch of tortellini for me and macaroni for Geoffrey, which both looked and tasted the same, we examine the crappy souvenirs in the adjacent gift shop, a mandatory part of any tour, and decide we do not need a black lava statue of a rearing horse or an ambling elephant, although we are tempted by the black lava Madonna. The woman behind the souvenir counter doesn't just take a step back when I ask her how much an ugly black and twisted milk jug with a fiery red rim is: she jumps back. I am now convinced people are startled by us because Geoffrey and I look like big Russians, but when we open our mouths out come broad Australian accents. It obviously unnerves people. I can't think of another theory, can you?

On the way back we all settle into dopey slumber, as you do when you are on a bus after a tour and lunch, and thank you, thank you God, Franco Woman goes into a deep sleep. Even the leader with four languages goes quiet. Geoffrey snores gently.

The middle-aged woman from Cornwall is right behind us again with her husband and he is very taken with the music coming softly through the overhead speakers. As soon as a tune comes on, he hums the first few bars and says to his wife, 'That be "Come Back To Sorrento", that be,' to which she replies 'Aarrgh.'

Another song.

'That be "O Sole Mio", that be.'

'Aarrgh.'

'That be "Arrivederci Roma", that be,' he continues. I am hooked now, and ready to say 'Aarrgh', but his wife beats me to it.

The next one has him puzzled for a while, until he works out the beat.

'That be "Granada", that be.'

'Aarrgh,' his wife and I reply in unison.

The next one completely flummoxes him … and me.

'What that be?' he says to his wife in an annoyed voice.

'Aarrgh,' says his wife, who has obviously not really listened properly to anything he's said in decades.

'Oh, that be that ice-skating song,' he finally says.

'Aarrgh.'

The three of us go quiet trying to think of the name of that bloody song, the one the ice-skating couple, Torvill and Dean, skated to so often. We can't remember its name—it doesn't come to me until later that evening. It's Ravel's 'Bolero'—but I'm sure you knew that, didn't you? Come on, say you did. Say 'Aarrgh.'

'There is a beautiful walk to a hilltop town above Taormina called Castelmola,' our driver had told us the night we arrived in Sicily. 'Castelmola is a lovely little town and there is a café there where the owner has a collection of unusual things, very … how do you say? … male things.'

That was enough to get me to talk Geoffrey into walking up to Castelmola. And a chatty young man at the information centre told us it was an easy walk, even though we could see Castelmola way up in the sky, a little village clinging for dear life to the top of a stupendous mountain.

'We'll take a bus up and walk back,' Geoffrey the Wise said. And just as well, too. Castelmola is 550 metres above sea level and the bus ride around the hairpin bends is fantastic, with terrifying sheer drops on one side.

Castelmola is well known for its almond wine, has a dwindling population, and sits on top of a rock with a ruined Byzantine castle. That much we know from the guidebook, but it hasn't told us how pretty it is. We stop in the small square to take in the fabulous views of Mt Etna and the Bay of Naxos and then branch off down the narrow roads looking for the café with the male things. We find it in the Piazza Duomo: it's called Caffe Turrisi, and is a narrow building of great character on five levels.

Penis enviers have no place inside this café. They confront you (the penises, not the enviers) from every corner and cranny in the crowded café, right from your first step inside the doors. The owner must surely have the largest collection in the world of penis ornaments, statues, adornments, sculptures, effigies, paintings and bric-a-brac under one roof. Think phallic and it is here. We seek out the owner, and for once, someone does not do a double take as we approach him. (When you think about it, anyone who owns several thousand penises can cope with anything and anybody.)

'Have you been collecting long?' I ask, pointing to a two-metre-high figure of a wizard sitting cross-legged with a three-metre-long penis rearing from beneath his skirts.

'My grandfather began the collection in 1921,' he says, and tells us all the memorabilia was collected locally. I think our English–Sicilian may have got a little confused, because I find it impossible to believe that such a huge and varied collection could be found on such a small island. Surely every corner of the earth must have been scoured to find the number and variety of penises inside this building?

'Take your time, look around, have a coffee,' the owner says in welcome. We need no further invitation.

Apart from the obvious large statues and wooden carved figures with gigantic organs, there are cabinets full of pink plastic penis objects, from drinking straws (think about that one, ladies) to candles and water jugs with penis handles. Penises are on every counter and shelf, in paintings and plaques on the walls, carved into the backs of chairs, twisted into the iron staircase rails, in every nook in the wall and every small corner of this incredible café. We explore every level, sitting on penis chairs (don't think too hard about that one) sipping our coffee from penis cups, looking out over the small balconies to the magic scene of the narrow street below. And when we think we have spotted every penis in the place we find more—a rooftop fountain with a delightful arrangement of upstanding willies stacked around a rearing centrepiece spurting water. Then yet more penises are painted on the mosaic tiles on the tabletops; penises stand up decoratively around a punch bowl, form the base of lampshades—and then, the *piece de resistance*, a monstrous wooden penis the size of a cannon, sits arrogantly along the length of a long wooden table in a large alcove. To give you more of an image here, hundreds of people have carved their names in this big beauty—does that paint a picture of its size and girth? I laugh until I almost pee, and a visit to the loo brings yet more penis delight: I enter by grabbing a brass penis door handle (in relaxed mode; think about that and you'll get the picture), and turn on the solid brass testicle taps to have water gushing from the curved phallic spout. It's marvellous.

On the rooftop terrace, surrounded by penis-shaped pots with pink geraniums growing festively from their tops, we look out over rooftops to a magnificent bell tower so close across the chasm of the street that we could almost poke out a penis and touch it. Geoffrey isn't willing to try, though. Coming back down the narrow staircase we have to duck, limbo style, to get beneath a long wooden penis thrusting from a small carved figure in an alcove in the wall—it reaches across the entire width of staircase.

Signing the penis-shaped visitors' book beside a penis-shaped beer tap, trying to think of something phallically witty to write, we read other notations. A German visitor has written 'Grotere Penissen Danin Belgie'; you can go look that up in your German dictionary if you can be bothered. I couldn't. I rather liked the sound of it as it was.

I can't imagine why, but I felt exhilarated when we left the Caffe Turrisi—I can only give this place the highest recommendation should you ever find yourself in Sicily. But plan to stay a long time, have a lazy lunch, and explore every little part of this quirky café.

We wander around the little village of Castelmola, now closing down for siesta, and explore the ruins of the old castle, leaning into a turret to take in the wide views of rooftops, cypress trees, olive groves, roads winding in the distance and the sapphire sea, but like other castles we have romped over (how good does that sound?) it smells as if a million men have peed on its old walls, and we can't stay too long.

The sky is very blue and we are up so high that it is quiet and hazy and beautiful, but it's also hot, so we decide we've had enough of a good thing up here in Castelmola and it's time to walk back down. The path is so steep we have to lean back to stop ourselves falling, but it's marvellous walking around the winding track past tall hollyhocks and old fig trees. Steep steps that leave our muscles aching punctuate the path; how anyone thought we could have walked up this is beyond imagination. When we reach the bottom our legs are jelly-like and we are ready for siesta ourselves.

For the next twenty-four hours everything I touch takes on a penis dimension. My water bottle, the big wooden tag on the hotel room key, a bottle of wine—I even call Geoffrey a penis head when he gets in my way. But in an endearing way, of course.

IN THE GARDENS
IN SICILY

A chapter about Sicily wouldn't be complete without a Mafia story, now would it? Unfortunately, I don't have one. But I am interviewing a woman today who surely will. Her name is Ellen Grady and she is the mother of the man who drove us from the airport (and hasn't he turned out to be good value?). Ellen is an English lady who came to Sicily forty-two years ago to teach English and escape the weather. In true Mills & Boon style she fell madly in love with a handsome Sicilian, married him, and has stayed forever in sunny Sicily. I want to interview her because she is author of the *Blue Guide Sicily*, a book that has helped us find our way around town and given us much enjoyment as well as information.

I meet Ellen for our interview in the Villa Schuler's lush gardens, and we sit in a small nook surrounded by lemon, almond and loquat trees, with the smell of jasmine in the air. I should explain that I have a friend who has a radio travel program in Australia called 'Around the World', and two minutes before I left for this trip he thrust a microphone and tape recorder at me and asked me to get some interviews for his show.

Ellen is a charming and informative woman who tells me her story in an articulate and structured manner, which is more than I can say for my interviewing technique.

When I play the tape back later, I hear myself gushing 'That's wonderful' after everything Ellen has said. I get uncomfortable about pauses and silences, you see, and have a compulsion to charge in with a 'That's wonderful' at every slight hesitation, even when Ellen tells me her son witnessed a Mafia murder when he was a young boy.

'He went out to buy bread and there was a horse race in the street,' Ellen says into the microphone. 'The Mafia didn't like the winner—he was supposed to have taken a fall, so they shot him and the horse bolted off fifty kilometres to the next town, dragging the dead man with him, and my son saw it all.'

'That's wonderful,' I scream into the microphone and then say something else that I have said a dozen times before and that annoys me to distraction: 'Now tell me ...'

I start every sentence with 'Now tell me ...' This, along with my 'That's wonderfuls', is the reason I am a writer not a radio broadcaster. But Ellen does tell me. All sorts of wonderful things.

She said that Giovanni Falcone, the magistrate who led an investigation into the Mafia—and who was himself assassinated in 1992—said there were more than 5000 'men of honour' in Sicily at the time. They controlled Sicilian business transcations through their legendary protection systems for many years and were true professional criminals obeying their own rigorous rules.

Things got really bad in the 1980s when many of Sicily's top business and professional people, including magistrates and poiticians, found the courage from somewhere deep inside and sood up to the Mafia, and were killed by the organistaion.

A courageous journalist by the name of Guisepe Fava challenged the Mafia in his newspaper, *I Siciliani*, and was killed for his trouble.

You can only imagine the fear of decent ordinary citizens of Sicily who were trying to go about their business. Who in their right mind would dare to challenge such an organised and ruthless gang?

But a brave group of shopkeepers and tradesmen in Cape d'Orlando did challenge them. They united and took such a strong stand they even got to court, which gave courage to other shop-keepers and tradespeople and ordinary Sicilians.

In 1987 many Mafia honchos were actually brought to trail and convicted, which was a small battle won, but (and I'd guess this was typical in Sicily because it is in every other group and committee in the world) internal fighting and conflict between the good guys meant their stand was no longer so united.

At one point it became so bad the Italian army was sent in to help. But according to Ellen, the Mafia made its biggest mistake in the late 1990s when it killed too many good people. Sicilians had finally had enough and became very angry and the Mafia lost a great deal of its standing at this time.

'I'm not saying they are not still here and active,' she said, 'but they are not nearly as powerful as they were.'

I try to draw more personal stories out of her with my pleas of 'Now tell me ...' and 'That's wonderful.' She is very cautious, but does give a little insight as to what she has noted over the past four decades.

'The Mafia probably started up in a difficult period for Sicily in the nineteenth century, when the economy was in crisis after World War II. The Mafia took control over the island, but in 1992 a lot of things happened at once and they lost ground. When they killed two magis-trates they got the whole population reacting against organised crime. Since then they have been trying to regain the hold they had on the population, but without much success. I'm not saying the Mafia is dead, because it is still there, but it is no longer as strong as it was in the past. Now people can invest in Sicily and they're looking to make tourism an important industry here, so hotels are being renovated and restored, and restaurants and factories making food products are sprouting up. Gradually the Mafia is being moved to one side. That's encouraging for this island. Buildings are being restored to their original beauty. There was a time in the 1950s, 1960s and even 1970s where a lot of mistakes were made—everybody went crazy about cement—but Italians are always Italians, and they are the masters when it comes to design. They have it in their blood, so now we are seeing beautiful places. Nobody is better than the Italians at restoring and refurbishing.'

I ask Ellen how she came to be an author and involved with *Blue Guide Sicily*.

'In the 1970s I was very concerned about what was happening in the world. I read *Silent Spring* by Rachel Carson and there was the Torrey Canyon disaster (where the oil tanker spill covered 25 000 birds in oil). I became involved in bird protection. Here in Sicily, anything that moved was being shot and eaten. It was terrible, so I started lobbying the MPs, and I was convincing. I managed to talk a few of them into backing plans for wildlife reserves—the first wildlife reserve in Sicily goes back to 1975. I was going to the newspapers, trying to get them to write articles about preserving wildlife, and they said, "Why don't you do it?" So I gradually became a journalist, a writer and a translator. I never dreamed of having a book of my own. It came quite by chance when I was asked to update the sixth edition of *Blue Guide Sicily*. It took two years of solidly working to completely update it, almost rewrite it.'

We talk for a while with the microphone off and I ask Ellen about her Sicilian family. Her husband is now dead, but she has a large family of in-laws and says family is very important to Sicilians—they spend as much time as possible with their family.

The conversation turns to the Greek Theatre and Ellen says she has seen many thrilling concerts there.

'In the 1950s it was decided to use the theatre to present a film festival, and if you look carefully you can see how well the Italians refurbished the theatre. It was a big success from the word go, and people like Rita Hayworth and Cary Grant and Joan Crawford and

Greta Garbo and Clarke Gable came. Taormina was renowned for the film festival. Now the film festival is no longer as important, but it is still held every June. After that we have a whole series of wonderful events, part of the Taormina Arts Festival. We had Nureyev dancing there. These are things you never forget. Two years ago I was there for the Bob Dylan concert. To watch a show or listen to music in the Greek Theatre is just fantastic.'

Now Ellen is about to embark on producing another *Blue Guide*, this time about a region in Italy called The Marches (pronounced Mar-kay), a blotch shape that clings to the east side of Umbria. It's full of history, churches, castles and medieval towns, and Ellen believes The Marches will be the Next Big Thing, more popular than Tuscany and Umbria put together.

Don't forget, you read it here first.

Every morning Geoffrey sits in his black underpants on the balcony and reads, and I write at my desk just inside the French doors. It's a simple routine that gives me much pleasure. I look up to the beautiful framed view (of the gardens and Mt Etna, not Geoffrey) and Greece seems very far away. The Villa Schuler really is handsome. It has marble-topped staircases and a dusky pink façade with deep green wrought iron rails around small balconies, and its gardens are lush and full of bird life—we can thank Ellen for that.

As the evenings close in we watch the alfresco restaurants on the ter-raced hills just above us come alive as waiters fuss about setting tables, watering geraniums in pots and calling out instructions. It is so peaceful just sitting and watching them, we have to force ourselves to shower and dress to go out. We know it is time to go back to Greece, but the temp-tation to stay is strong. We have spent many long days swimming and laz-ing on the beaches, turning down offers from the poor African men tramping barefoot on the hot sand with their beaming smiles and bags of junk, and in the evenings we have wandered all over Taormina discovering small restaurants and little cafés of great appeal.

At the Ristorante Ciglope on the main Corso, we sat a table right at the edge of the street and ate tagliatelle with tuna and black olives and veal scaloppini, and listened to a roving group of young men dressed in black shorts and white shirts playing the piano accordion, flute and tambourine, and even blowing a tune across the top of a colourfully painted jug. After one jovial bout at the entrance to the restaurant, they stopped playing and passed around the jug, shaking it under the faces of the diners for tips. One tune and they want money? When people refused they acted as if they didn't care and threw the jug theatrically in the air before catching it and wandering to the next restaurant to try to rip off someone else. We see them again the next night as we sit at a table balanced on the steps of a tiny café in a back street and eat spaghetti bolognese and pizza. After only one tune again, around comes the jug; most people throw money into it this time, but not us.

We wander each night along the Corso Umberto with hundreds of others and stop at the Wunderbar—another place that Ava, Liza and Richard partied at—and listen to a man playing 'Autumn Leaves' on the organ. It sounds odd, but is in fact very charming.

Time passes far too quickly and now we must leave Taormina and spend a couple of days in the capital, Palermo. And then it is definitely back to Greece.

We have a small adventure on the way to Palermo: our bus fills with smoke and the driver makes us all get off. We are on the busy autostrada, and one overweight old lady (not me) cannot make the small jump over the railing at the side of the road to the safety of a grassed area, so we all have to make a fireman's chair with our hands and lift her. It isn't attractive. Our driver aims the fire extinguisher at the big engine in the back of the bus for a few minutes while we all stand around and gape, then he tells us to get back on the bus and we proceed without explanation—or, indeed, further problems—to Palermo. We form an intense dislike of Palermo the minute we enter the city: there are ugly high-rise apartments with unsightly air-conditioners and satellite dishes hanging off them and washing flapping everywhere.

We trundle our bags down the hot and dirty street from the bus terminal and a tiny man leaps out at us with offers of a taxi. It is obviously not a taxi—it is his own car, and has a dirty old towel wrapped around its decrepit front seat, secured with a safety pin at the back. We don't care; we are anxious for transport. There is no air-conditioning or taxi meter, but the little man is helpful and lifts our enormous cases into the boot, and we don't mind how uncomfortable the trip to our hotel is as long as we get away from these unlovely city streets.

We have no idea why we are staying outside Palermo at Monreale. The man at the Villa Schuler—obviously delighted to see us leave—had booked this hotel for us. We do not know what to expect, or indeed what Monreale is all about. Well, it turns out to be completely bloody wonderful. But not at first. Our hotel is at the end of a series of constricted streets that our little taxi man has navigated carefully, almost scraping the sides of buildings. He then charged us 93 euros for what we find out later should have been a 35 euro trip. The hotel is not grand and our room is small and mean and puts us in a dark mood, but it does have a fabulous view from the balcony out over the city to rolling brown hills beyond. There is nowhere to sit in the room apart from on the bed, and we don't know what to do at three in the afternoon, so we go grumpily out for a walk. The streets are cobbled and narrow with old houses and apartments facing right onto the tight streets and we catch glimpses through net curtains of families eating or at rest in tiny rooms.

Just as we are both thinking how unappealing this place is, we come to a large square of great charm, filled with fountains and milling people, and, towering grandly over it all, a stunning cathedral. Our mood lifts immediately. Of course it is a famous cathedral and people have come from all over the world to see it, and here we are, by chance staying at a hotel down the road—and we have never heard of it. Even the hotel receptionist had not told us about it when we left for our walk. We feel ridiculous. 'Monreale is world-renowned for this cathedral, a dazzling mixture of Arab, Byzantine and Norman artistic styles framed by traditional Romanesque architecture', we read from a leaflet as we enter the fabulous building.

'Monreale's mosaics emblazon 6340 square metres of the cathedral's interior surface, more than those of the splendid church of Saint Mark in Venice.' Better than the one in Venice? Now that is pretty awesome, *and we have just chanced upon it.* We go quiet before such beauty, and sit on the pews while the tourists flock all around us with cameras and notebooks. There is not a square centimetre of wall or ceiling without a mosaic, each one depicting a story of tragedy or enlightenment. There's a man with dropsy getting divine intervention. We stare at that for many minutes and then look at Adam and Eve. Adam and Eve, all gold leaf paint, and so high up on the walls we have to crane our necks right back to look. We can't find an English-speaking tour group to latch on to so we wander round by ourselves, suitably agog, and put a euro into one of those little machines with a phone and press the English language button. A woman on the other end gives us a longwinded history which would no doubt be full of interesting facts if only we did not lose interest after the opening sentence about the cathedral being built at the order of William II in 1153.

When we are all gaped out we leave through massive solid wooden doors, and explore the streets leading off the square before buying a book about Monreale. Monreale is located on the slope of Mt Caputo, about seven kilometres south of Palermo's centre (93 euros for a seven-kilometre taxi ride, remember?) and has about 25000 residents. It overlooks the Conca d'Ora, the beautiful valley beyond Palermo—that's the view from our little hotel room—and we are approximately 300 metres above sea level. We are always finding ourselves in places high above sea level, aren't we?

We decide we like Monreale very much. It abounds with colourful fruit and vegetable shops full of purple eggplants and the brightest red tomatoes we've come across yet. Pastry shops with tempting tortes, and delis with huge hams and cheeses are plentiful. Later we look in our guidebook and read an old Italian proverb. 'He who goes to Palermo without visiting Monreale, goes as a donkey and returns as a beast.' We certainly qualify as donkeys for coming to this historic place without knowing a thing about it.

At this time Monreale is festooned with pink and black flags. They're everywhere—strung across the streets, hanging outside shops, waving from houses, fluttering from car aerials. It has to be Palermo's football team obviously about to play an important match, and we determine to find out. We see a crowd of people ahead blocking the street and Geoffrey insists we run after them to see what is happening, because he thinks it's a Mafia funeral. We catch up with the crowd, and it is indeed a funeral. Smartly dressed men in black and woman in tailored suits and high heels are walking behind a big hearse, but no-one seems to be crying or looking in the least distressed.

'Mafia, it just has to be Mafia,' Geoffrey says, all excited—blokes do get carried away by Mafia stories—and we join in the funeral march until we get bored and wander off on our own to poke around the shops a little more.

Back at the hotel I brace myself to enter the hot, claustrophobic bathroom. An attempt has been made at modernisation: the owners have installed a shower in the tight corner, but its base is the size of my oven tray back home, and once the shower curtain is pulled around, it clings to my body like a slimy second skin. The shower apparatus itself is a portable modern thing with a fireman's hose pressure and a life of its own. It leaps off its socket, whirls around like a crazed snake and blasts me with stinging force, then sends the curtain into a flapping frenzy that slaps and slides into crevices you don't want to hear about.

At the end of the shower the bathroom resembles a small swimming pool. The bidet is full, the toilet is drenched, the sink is awash, my wash bag is soaked, and all the towels are saturated. Even the toilet roll is soggy and squashed. It comes adrift and floats out on a soapy river into the bedroom, which gives Geoffrey something to think about before I come out, battered and bruised, to dry myself on the bedspread.

A BRUSH
WITH THE MAFIA?

Two friendly men run our hotel and now that they are used to us, and have got over their initial startled reaction, they are relaxed in our company. We ask them about the pink and black flags hanging up in the town.

'An important football match being played in Napoli,' they said. 'Palermo is in the finals for the first time in thirty-two years. Everyone has gone football crazy. It is a very big time for us.'

They recommend a restaurant—Mizzica—just off the square near the cathedral and we set off for dinner. Just down the road we pass an ornate mansion guarded by five fierce Alsatians; they rush to the gates and bare their ferocious fangs at us. We scramble past quickly and immediately come across an old bent-over woman walking a tiny white toy poodle that looks like a cotton ball and is wearing a muzzle.

'You have to love this place,' Geoffrey says.

It is Saturday night, and every one of the 25000 citizens of Monreale seems to be out. Attractive young girls with their flat brown bellies showing, and handsome young men with heavily gelled hair cluster around parked Vespas giggling and flirting. Pre-teens race around the square and elegant women link arms and do circuit after circuit around the fountain, while old men sit in the surrounding cafés looking over the happy scene.

We sit for a short while on the edge of the fountain and then in a café, where we sip white wine and let the feeling of family contentment here in Monreale have its way with us.

Finally, we go searching for Mizzica in the back streets and get lost in the maze. We can find no trace of any restaurants at all, and we wander on and on until we stumble on a narrow door to a restaurant, and a blackboard that announces: 'Panoramic views and a tourist menu'. We give up on our original plan.

The restaurant is on two levels and we climb up creaky old stairs to the rooftop garden where the waiters, still setting up for the evening, look at us as though we are creatures just risen from a black lagoon.

A table? You have actually come in here expecting dinner? their looks say, and after we assure them that yes, we do want dinner and will pay them money for it, they reluctantly give us a table. But it is a good table, pushed right up against the railings, where red geraniums flourish in pots and the view is indeed panoramic—we can see across to the surrounding hills, dotted with grand villas, and out over to the sprawling city of Palermo, where the early evening light is turning everything soft pink.

The waiters are arguing angrily with each other, moving tables noisily and scraping chairs loudly. There is no-one else in the restaurant yet and they ignore us. It is not a welcoming atmosphere and we try to block them out and concentrate on the tourist menu, which isn't very tourist-friendly because it doesn't have a word of English on it. My limited Italian helps me guess and we order penne carbonara, pesto spaghetti, a risotto with four cheeses, a cuttlefish salad and a carafe of house wine. The unhelpful waiter tells us there is no house wine available today and we want to accuse him of lying—because there is always house wine in Sicily—but we don't dare. Instead we let him guide us to a bottle of the most expensive wine, and fume to ourselves. The waiters continue arguing, fussing angrily over a long table just behind us, repeating the name 'Capitano' over and over. This excites us. A visit by the Mafia will make for an interesting story, which I promise to relate to you. However, the restaurant fills with mostly innocent-looking tourists and the long table behind us remains empty.

The lights start to twinkle all over the hills—the setting is utterly gorgeous, but the service and food are quite appalling. Finally the Capitano arrives and takes the head of the table behind us. He is not a swarthy man wearing a black shirt and white tie with a coat slung rakishly over his shoulders, but instead a thirteen-year-old boy, celebrating his birthday. He has a crowd of other thirteen-year-old boys with him (all bearing gifts) and two doting parents, draped with so much video equipment they could be shooting a Steven Spielberg spectacular.

The rude waiters become obsequious around this boy and fuss over him, taking the five hundred birthday presents his parents have brought with them and putting them carefully on a sideboard, arranging his pink and black flag on the back of his chair which he promptly removes and ties around his head, Rambo style.

My penne is a gluggy mess, Geoffrey's pesto is thin and tasteless, and the salad is bereft of any cuttlefish at all but has a generous scattering of canned corn on limp lettuce. The table of boys behind us gets louder and louder and mamma and papa capture every moment of the party on video, circling the table with cameras on their shoulders, issuing instructions for the boys to turn this way and that. My risotto arrives and is like a soggy rice pudding. It is by far the most awful thing I can recall eating in years. But we drink our wine and listen to the noise around us with a pleasant feeling of being part of Monreale life. Now the view is in full night-time mode, with the lights twinkling romantically.

When we have had enough we call for the bill and hand the surly waiter our credit card, which immediately brings forth a burst of indignation. 'No credit card accepted here,' he says. We tell him we had seen Visa and American Express signs on the window when we entered. He doesn't want a scene in the now-packed restaurant, so sends us downstairs to deal with the boss.

The bill is 61 euros; we have 20 euros cash only, plus an old 50 000 lira note. The boss, a dark, angry, short man, screams up to our faces when we say he has no choice but to take our card. He then screams to his wife, who in turn shouts to the pizza man, who then shouts at the kitchen hand, who barks at the dishwashing girl. It is horrible. Fortunately, there are no customers down here. The boss then runs to the front door and brings back a small scrap of paper—like a corner torn out of an exercise book—on which is scribbled 'credit card machine kaput' and demands to know why we hadn't noticed this blazingly obvious sign stuck on the window when we walked in.

'We do not have enough cash, so you tell us what to do,' Geoffrey says to him, which makes him even angrier. We have never felt so berated.

'Can I help in the kitchen?' I offer in my most pleasant manner, when really what I want to do is grab his testicles tightly and twist sharply.

'You pay, you pay, you pay,' he screams.

'Would you like this 50 000 lira note?' Geoffrey says, which tempts him for a moment—lira can still be changed for euros at Italian banks.

'No, then I'll have to go on the bus into Palermo because the bank in Monreale won't change it,' he says and starts shouting again at this wife, who shouts at the pizza man, who shouts at the kitchenhand, who shouts at the dishwashing girl.

There seems to be no solution to this problem—he will not trust us to leave and come back with cash in the morning—until we ask this dreadful little man to telephone our hotel, where the credit card machine is not kaput, and put the bill on our account there and get the hotel to reimburse him in cash.

More shouting follows, this time into the telephone, and finally we are allowed to leave. We feel like naughty children. As we walk back, we find that what were empty streets several hours earlier are now action-packed streets, with hundreds of people sitting at tables and chairs at appealing restaurants that have sprung up from nowhere.

'All these choices and we had to get the one nasty bastard in Monreale,' I say to Geoffrey.

'It's because we ate too early: you have to wait until 9 pm or 10 pm here before the restaurants put out their tables and chairs,' he replies.

Back at our hotel, after running the gauntlet of the fang-bearing Alsatians at the mansion again, our kind reception man sympathises with our problem at the restaurant, and although he has little English, he manages to impart that perhaps their credit card machine was not really, how you say? kaput.

I whispered 'Mafioso' to Geoffrey in the background, and the man immediately picks it up and agrees wholeheartedly. He indicates that yes, in fact Mafioso machinations were most likely at work there; it was probably in order to avoid paying tax that the skunk said the machine was broken.

'He is crazy man, no good,' he says. 'Why you not go to our recommendation?'

We tell him we couldn't find it, which seems stupid now.

'We never recommend that man's restaurant to our guests,' he says. 'All he has is the panoramic view. His food is no good. Mafioso, very bad here. And that big house down the road with the dogs—Mafioso too.'

I am now convinced that the Mafioso will come looking for us through the night. Broken legs and horses' heads will be with us by morning. I set about securing the doors and windows in our small room, frightening myself as a child does. Geoffrey couldn't care less; he gets stuck into the brandy out on the balcony, admiring the fabulous view by night, until I finally call him in. Although our room has a formidable steel shutter at the balcony door with a massive lock at the window, it has no air-conditioning and we are forced to leave the doors open. I set silly traps—suitcases, chairs, my big shoes and fearsome bras placed in front of the window to trip up axe-wielding Mafia murderers carrying bleeding horses' heads into the room.

It all seems so stupid in the bright light of the morning as we sit in the downstairs lounge, surrounded by antique furniture and grand paintings eating buttery croissants and juicy peaches.

'We really must get back to Greece,' Geoffrey says. 'I do like this place, but I couldn't stand another night in that horrible room.'

'Me neither. Let's get out of Sicily.'

And the Palermo football team lost 3–0.

It takes us the entire day to get back to Greece, even though it is just a short hop from Sicily. We have a long wait at the Palermo airport and a stopover in Rome, which puts the wind up me. I have an unreasonable fear of airports. Not of terrorists or shoe bombers. It's a terror of getting locked in the toilet and missing my plane. It happened to me once and I have yet to get over it. I always check airport toilets for an escape route before I close the door. Could I squeeze over the partition into the next cubicle if I got locked in? Could I crawl under the door? If the toilet has walls and a door that go right to the ceiling I refuse to use it.

The toilets at Palermo airport are so swish and modern that the doors shut and lock on you by themselves the minute you enter, and the toilet seat remains up, as if a bloke has just used it. It also flushes by itself, which is most disconcerting, because it doesn't do it when you want it to and you either cop a Niagara Falls-like gush of water on your soft parts before you've finished, or you get up and nothing at all happens, which isn't going to be pretty for the person who follows you. It is in here that I get stuck, with the toilet deciding not to flush and then changing its mind a good five minutes later as I struggle with the lock on the door. I am at the stage of crying now, and am thinking of calling for help—although the idea of being an old lady locked in the lavatory again is a humiliation beyond bearing—when the door automatically opens, the toilet lid springs up and the Niagara Falls flushes start all over again.

On the plane from Rome to Athens, which is full of Italians—going to Greece for a holiday, presumably—they show a stupid video called *Just For Laughs*, where people get set up in all sorts of weird situations, and their reactions are caught on hidden cameras. I have never before seen an entire planeload of people so enjoying the in-flight entertainment. Italians appear to love to laugh at just about anything—and good on them too. This show is obviously one of their favourites.

Every passenger explodes into hysterical laughter as some idiot posing as a gay policeman gives people parking tickets and a feel-up at the same time. And when a man pushes a dummy in a wheelchair into a manhole in front of horrified onlookers, a tide of laughter surges through the plane. Ditto for the man who pulls a carpet of fake grass over himself and slinks, worm-like, over the lawns in a popular park to people sitting on benches to grab their ankles and frighten the hell out of them. The Italians shriek with glee.

Actually, to be truthful, so do I.

BACK TO THE ISLANDS

My, but it took a long time to get to Sifnos. Two planes, a taxi, a metro ride and a long trip on a ferry, and finally we are here.

Sifnos is the fourth island in the Western Cyclades. It is small and mountainous, with fertile valleys, and has been inhabited since 3000 BC. There are hundreds of churches sprinkled all over the island, and its main activity centres around the large Bay of Kamares.

'Visually attractive and still Greek,' we read on the internet. 'Great beaches, fantastic food. The Port of Kamares is the cleanest port in the entire Aegean.'

We are at this cleanest port in the Aegean right now, disembarking with a hundred others. 'Sifnos is one of the most unspoilt of all the Greek islands,' we have also been promised, and this excites us. However, it is not so unspoilt as to not have all the comforts necessary for a woman such as me to enjoy herself—plenty of pleasant hotels, small cafés, unpretentious shops, and little fishing villages with beachside tavernas galore for her to sit in, drinking wine and eating food. Magical.

'There is no Mykonos-style partying here; no glam Santorini crowd,' I later write in my diary. 'This place is about family-owned hotels, and beachside tavernas where the legs of your chair sink lower into the sand as you fill up on the fishermen's bounty of the day.'

I rather like the sound of these notes, if I say so myself.

The Hotel Stavros, which is to be our home for the next month, is just 100 metres from the port and right on the waterfront, among shops and cafés. This is a good thing for us now, as we wheel heavy suitcases off the ferry, but could well be a bad thing in the middle of the night. We knew this hotel was right in the heart of the port when we booked it from Australia, but the pictures on the internet looked so pretty, with the charming brick building facing the water, the bustling cafés below it and the views over the bay to the lofty brown mountains, that we took a chance. The owner, a super friendly man called Stavros, had been so obliging via email, and with the price an agreeably low 35 euros a night, we thought we could put up with a bit of noise in the night.

And Stavros indeed turns out to be every bit as friendly as we'd hoped he would be. He does not leap back when we walk into his reception area, nor does he ask for passports or credit cards. He smiles, shakes hands, takes our bags, shows us to our big room and tells us to enjoy ourselves and he'll see us in the morning. It's about ten in the evening and very lively downstairs. I tramp around the room fussing about the noise from the cafés, stressing about the motor scooters zooming past on the small road separating the hotel from the beach. Although it is a picture of absolute Greek charm outside our window, one thing is obvious—it is going to be noisy during the night.

And it is.

We simply cannot sleep with the old Greek men arguing happily in the café until two in the morning and the young Greek men revving their scooters until three.

But in the light of the morning, we see that the view is even better as we look out to those beautiful brown mountains curving magnificently around the bay. However, I am determined to ask Stavros if we can leave. Geoffrey doesn't want to offend this friendly man or take this long booking away from him.

'Stavros was born on the island,' I tell Geoffrey. 'His family is bound to own other properties. I'm sure he'll have something else. I don't want to take my business away from him, I just want to take it somewhere quieter.'

Well, all I can say is—and believe me, I do—thank goodness Geoffrey has me.

It turns out Stavros has a villa (belonging to his mother, who has conveniently been removed from her home into another one of his hotels) high up on the hill right behind us and it is available and ready for our pleasure for as long as we want for a mere 45 euros a night. It has an even better view than from the hotel, and is only a matter of ten (hard puffing) minutes up steps from the beachfront. A large living room, fully equipped kitchen, big bedroom, spacious bathroom and a gloriously long veranda overlooking the Bay of Kamares are all ours for the next month.

'And you didn't want to upset Stavros,' I gloat to Geoffrey as he pours pre-lunch gin and tonics and we pull up chairs at the table on our private veranda to better gaze out to the most beautiful view in the world.

The villa is built into a rocky cliff, so no-one looks down on us. We can see clear across the blue bay to those mountains that remind me of a giant roller-coaster, and out to sea, where the big ferries come in several times a day. This veranda becomes our most beloved spot over the next month; a place where we idle hours away and gaze in awe at the dramatic sunsets every evening. A place where we linger in the mornings eating yoghurt drenched in honey and covered with nuts. Where we sip wine in the early evenings as the village below quietens down. This is the place where Geoffrey turns a deep brown and lies on a sunlounge for long hot afternoons in his skimpy black underpants. A place where I sit in a shady spot and read book after book borrowed from Stavros's library. This is our dearly loved veranda in our whitewashed blue-shuttered villa high on the hill. It's a Greek island fantasy and could possibly be pretentious if it wasn't for a nightly parade of scruffy goats passing our door. These adorable creatures go past each night, stopping to munch on grass by the road and giving us a once-over stare. They bring us down to earth and have us running for the camera.

'How can we possibly ever leave this place?' we sigh every morning as we wake to our view, and again in the evenings as we emerge fresh and damp from the shower to pull up a chair on our beloved veranda. 'This place has moved itself into my soul,' I tell Geoffrey, who just grunts—I suspect he feels the same way too but doesn't like saying schmaltzy stuff like that.

We shop in the tiny supermarket next door to Stavros's hotel—it is owned by Stavros's sister (I told you his family would own just about everything on this island)—buying black olives, red tomatoes, purple onions and white fetta from a young man who gathers these goodies from baskets, boxes and deep silver tins on the floor. Most days, after our Greek salad lunch on our veranda we walk down to the beach and around the Bay of Kamares, a 400 metre sweep of soft sand and shallow water. We look back up to our villa, sitting white and pretty up on the hill, and feel damn smug. It is possible to walk for many hundreds of metres out in the shallow water of the bay, which makes it perfect for children, and when the large ferries sweep into the port in the distance they create waves that rush forcefully to the shore and delight the frolicking children. The town of Kamares is tucked around the edge of the bay, at the bottom of the mountains. Its buildings are white with blue shutters, in the typical Cyclades style, but are square, and without domes.

Close up those beautiful brown mountains are hard and rocky structures covered in a few tufts of green. Two are topped with white monasteries, Agios Simeon and Profitis Ilias, tiny dots high in the high distance.

We find a delightful swimming spot at the bottom of the rocks on this other side of the bay and clamber with difficulty down to the tiny rocky cove; there's no-one around so we take all our clothes off and sink into the deep clear water. It is indescribably good after the heat of the walk. When we're refreshed and dressed we climb awkwardly back up and then wander around the road at the top. We come to a huge new house, obviously empty, jutting out over the rocks and overlooking the bay. We trespass onto the wide veranda, peek through the windows to covered furniture and then sit on the veranda walls as if we own them, and watch the ferries come in. They spew out hundreds of people, cars, trucks and scooters and then depart, all within a few minutes. People say the Greek transport and infrastructure generally is terrible, but as far as we have seen, these ferries are super efficient, always on time to the minute, and in and out of port admirably quickly.

We return to our side of the bay and stop at a beachside taverna. We sit on chairs out on the sand, beneath tamarisk trees, and eat fried cheese and drink red wine.

'I could easily become a Greek,' I say after a big mouthful of greasy cheese. Although all menus in all tavernas have been stupendously repetitious in our experience, we have come to enjoy certain things—the honey/yoghurt breakfast, the daily Greek salad lunch, and now this devilishly fattening fried cheese.

Everywhere we have travelled in the past we end up with a few favourite dishes, and when we return to Australia, we faithfully cook their cuisine for the next few months, so taken are we with the whole food and travel connection. After our trip to Italy we lived on spaghetti and pesto for six weeks. After Thailand I could cook nothing but red duck curry and pad Thai for a full month. But once the novelty wears off, we forget all about our new culinary passions and rarely cook such things again. In Switzerland once we bought a nifty gadget we could not live without at the time, a round silver thing with prongs on it that you sat your apple on and pushed down hard so that it swiftly and neatly quartered the apple—so typical of the Swiss to even go about apple eating in an efficient and clean way. When we returned to Australia we went on an apple-eating orgy, quartering apples at all hours of the day and sometimes during the night, until the fun of our apple quarterer faded and we threw the gadget in the kitchen drawer and never gave it another thought until a year later, when cleaning out the drawers one day, Geoffrey pulled the thing out and said (rather eloquently I thought), 'What the fuck's this?' It is the way with most things purchased abroad. I'm sure you too have a drawer full of fabulously useless things that you have forgotten you ever bought.

So now we look forward to endless Greek salads and fried cheese when we return to Australia.

We hire a zippy red motor scooter. Stavros has given us a map and told us the island has many small bays suitable for swimming. With our increased scooter confidence and the fairly traffic-free roads of Sifnos, we zoom happily along, me sitting up straight on the back of the bike to look out at the surrounding countryside.

We pass olive trees, vineyards, and old men on donkeys. It is as unspoilt as you could ask for and really, when you think about it, I shouldn't be telling you much more about Sifnos—you'll probably crowd me out here next year.

In the main town of Apollonia we park the scooter and wander through the crazy-paved streets, full of whitewashed houses and little shops that open onto the street; it reminds us strongly of Mykonos, but without the crowds. We climb and puff our way up to the top of a hill and look out over the rolling hills to churches, churches, and more churches. We drive on to Plati Ghialos Bay on the southeast of the island, where cafés and small guesthouses line the beach. A German man we had seen on the ferry holding the hands of his two plump boys now plays in the water with them. We sit on the beach and read, and watch him throw a ball non-stop to the two boisterous boys and let them jump off his shoulders. His wife makes only brief appearances in the water.

I'm reading *Bella Tuscany* by Frances Mayes now, and I'm enchanted by it. If I had a single wish, it would be to have the talent to write the kind of evocative prose she does, to take my readers right into the heart of a place as she does.

The wind was so strong last night it woke me (while Geoffrey snored on) as it howled around our shutters and caused dogs to bark frantically in the distance. I lay in bed in the dark listening to the high-pitched wind, worrying that it would whip Geoffrey's underpants off the washing line and blow them all the way to Mykonos, where they would wrap themselves around the heads of a gay couple sitting in a café drinking Camparis. I consoled myself that at least the underpants were spiffy black bikini Calvin Kleins—the only kind I allow Geoffrey to wear.

We take hours to get ourselves organised in the mornings. We are on holiday, I know, but we are sure we're missing out on sunny morning scenes in the harbour. At home we always start our day with a 6 am walk. Here, we wake lazily around nine, throw back the blue shutters, and I then spend half an hour banging on about the fabulous view from the bed out to the roller-coaster hills with the white monasteries on top. Geoffrey brings in the tea and gets the honey and yoghurt ready, and then I get up and write my diary. Then we move out to the veranda, where I bang on for another half an hour about the roller-coaster hills with the monasteries on top. By the time we eat our yoghurt and have several cups of coffee it is creeping towards midday.

'We really should be walking; we haven't done a thing,' I say one morning after my fourth cup of coffee. 'The intention was to walk a lot here but I haven't worn my walking shoes even once.' Geoffrey often doesn't answer me, especially after I have banged on and on about monasteries on top of mountains. He believes answers are not necessary and most often they are not. I continue. 'We could walk up that mountain to visit that monastery.'

Which of course is probably the most profoundly stupid thing I have ever said, because Geoffrey immediately takes his nose out of the paper and says, 'Let's go—right now', and then delves into the suitcase for the walking shoes.

A MONASTERY ON TOP OF
A MOUNTAIN

Stavros has told us it is quite possible to walk to the monastery Agios Simeon by way of a goat track up the mountain. Geoffrey says I would never make it up five metres of goat track, let alone the 400 metres to the top, but might have a good chance if we take the road that winds more gently around the mountain.

We are suitably attired, wearing shoes, T-shirts, shorts and hats, and have sunscreen, water and a modest picnic lunch of bread, gorgonzola and tomatoes. Never mind that it is one o'clock in the afternoon before we take off—the hottest part of the day, when everyone else is thinking about closed blinds and cool siestas—we are going up the mountain.

The first 100 metres are easy: the road is bitumen and it rises only gradually. We plod upwards, looking back down to the patchwork landscape in the valleys. Small stone walls separate little farmed sections where attractive rolls of hay lie side by side. Olive trees are spread in neat patterns before us. There is no sign of cars here but plenty of donkey droppings, and we like it this way. The air becomes still and hotter as we climb.

We cross small precarious stone bridges over dry trenches and stop every fifteen minutes for swigs of water. Dry spiky thistles line the road, reminding me sharply of my childhood. These same thistles were common in the unlovely landscape of Sunshine in Melbourne where I grew up, and the sight of black-clad Greek widows bent over collecting these horrible things by the side of the roads in our miserable neighbourhood was common, and now flashes clearly back to me. As an English child growing up in Australia, I was a little confused and frightened by the many ethnic people with strange customs and habits surrounding me—none of these customs was ever explained to me, and I just accepted that old Greek ladies collected thistles from the roadsides for dinner.

'What part of the thistle would they eat?' I ask Geoffrey now. He himself is a person not averse to eating things straight from the ground. 'The inside of the flower bit,' he says. 'I imagine they boil them up like a vegetable.' He pokes around the desiccated flower part of a thistle and I walk on, because I really don't like to look at thistles, even for a moment. We climb and climb, and can see the white monastery seemingly miles away high in the distance. The bitumen runs out and we walk on a rocky, but wide, dusty track. The views become more dramatic by the minute, and the feeling of being so high is exciting. We have been walking for an hour and have not seen a person, nor sighted a car or a motor scooter. We are alone with our mountain and our monastery up in the heavens. It's pleasant, despite the heat.

Gone now are the ugly thistles, and instead wildflowers and herb bushes grow by the track and on the surrounding hills. Geoffrey is in his element, plucking flowers, sniffing herbs, asking botanical questions of himself—he knows I wouldn't know the answers. We pass little blue wooden boxes scattered among the rocks. Geoffrey, who was a budding beekeeper as a teenager until all his bees escaped one day and stung him from the top of his head to the end of his toes, recognises them instantly as beehives. This excites him further, because he's a bit of a nature boy at heart.

A rooster crows in the distance and we pass a donkey in an old wooden stable—the feeling of being in a remote, long-forgotten place intensifies. A ripe farmyard smell announces a goat farm long before we come to it. When we do, the curious goats run to the fence to stare at us with undisguised scorn, much as most hotel receptionists do.

'What is it about us that makes people and animals look at us like that?' I ask. Geoffrey has no answer. The goats follow us along their fence line, the bells around their necks clanging quite musically, belying their ugly stares.

The road flattens, which pleases us, as we are panting and red-faced now and regretting the Greek pastries we had along with our honeyed yoghurt this morning. Geoffrey becomes further excited about the variety of wild herbs growing near the road. Tufts of greenery sprout from rocks and dry patches all over the hard land. He picks off bits, sniffs them, eats them. He has always eaten things from the garden, even at home in our patch of suburban backyard in Australia. I always thought if I locked him out of the house he could probably survive for weeks without leaving our garden. Looking back over the years, I can remember him being in the garden for entire days, and every time I looked out of the kitchen window from my chores he was eating something. 'What on earth are you eating?' I would call out, because there didn't seem to me to be anything edible out there.

'Just a nasturtium leaf,' he'd say and reach for a hydrangea bush for a change of flavour. Summer was his favourite time, of course. We had fruit trees, lemon trees and grapevines, and carrots and onions in the ground, and there was glorious abundance at every turn. Apricots, plums, nectarines, washed down with a bit of straight lemon juice, could make Geoffrey a happy man. But he would also chomp away in the garden in the winter months, when the trees were bare and earth cold and infertile. You may think Geoffrey is strange, but I am here to tell you it is a fine thing to have a man who can eat anything. I cannot bear wimpy men who have strong food dislikes and search under their mashed potatoes in case someone has snuck a brussels sprout in there. Geoffrey is the kind of blokey bloke who can eat mouldy stuff going off in the fridge. Apart from eating flowers in the garden, he is at his happiest when I have my annual fridge clean out.

'Don't throw that out,' he says as I'm about to ditch yoghurt on the fizzy turn or a squishy tomato or unidentifiable leftovers. He gleefully warms up and gobbles up old stew, musty chicken and stale pasta. He cannot bear food waste—this is a legacy of his dear New Zealand mother. She never ever wasted a thing from her garden or fridge, and could make a filling meal out of just a small piece of meat and baskets of goodies from her vegetable plot. She was ahead of her time in many ways, especially in the recycling stakes: she used to wash jars and wrappings from bread bags for further use. I don't think she ate flowers, though. And I actually do clean my fridge out more than once a year.

Now, up on this organic Greek mountain, Geoffrey nibbles contentedly on oregano, rosemary and sage, and crushes bits in his fingers so that I can enjoy their herby smells. What a man!

We keep catching glimpses of the monastery in the distance as we follow the turns in the road, and for the first time it looks just a fraction closer. We think we must be nearing the halfway mark.

A lone brown horse up on a slope above us stares at us with a baleful look as we pass.

We are seriously high now, and looking back down on where we have walked; the land appears more fertile, more agriculturally friendly than the lower slopes. There are little bits sectioned off by beautiful stone walls into olive groves, grapevine fields, and small grazing areas for goats. The sky is hazy blue and there is an eerie shimmer over the mountains. The cicadas trill loudly as we make another water stop.

We reach a vast cavity, an old mineshaft, now turned into the local tip. It is an ugly scar on the lovely landscape, with rubbish clinging to the side of the crater where it has not fallen right down. There is the awful smell of burning rubber in the air and we hurry to pass this sacrilege. Still we have not come across another person—no farmer, backpacker, no goat keeper. We are the only people mad enough to be up here on this hot afternoon. By now we are three-quarters of the way up and can look right across to Apollonia, a cluster of white buildings, somnolent and peaceful against the blue of the distant sea.

Finally, a man approaches on a donkey, sitting side-saddle. It is a sight so quintessentially Greek, so *right* in this setting, that we want to embrace him. He stops, and we see he is very old and very weathered. He has not a word of English, yet he is friendly and happy to pose for our camera. He indicates that we are crazy to be walking so high up in this heat, but he doesn't stare at us as though we have two heads and we love him for it. After we take his picture we wonder if we should give him money and decide not to because it would be insulting. He waves goodbye and the donkey trots off. The man looks so proud and beautiful sitting side-saddle that we are glad we did not make the affronting offer.

Now hundreds of pretty yellow butterflies come out in the still air and surround us. As we walk through their fragile fluttery wings and glance down to the deep blue of the Aegean Sea, we wonder why more people are not up here enjoying this glorious mountain.

When we come to the last 100 metres the climb becomes more difficult, and we are forced to leave the road and take a precipitous rocky path.

At last, doubled over by the steepness of the track and our own exhaustion, we reach the monastery, a serene white Santorini-style building with a white dome and wide courtyard space. After we have straightened up and caught our breath, we almost lose it again. *The views.* We are so high, so vertical, that we feel we could topple right over and roll all the way down the mountain back to Kamares, tumbling over thistles and oregano and goat and donkey droppings. It is quite spectacular, and so vertiginous that we have to step back from the edge of the monastery walls and clutch each other to stop swaying.

To our delight, we find the door to the monastery open and we step inside. It is modestly decorated—a couple of gold pedestals, a chandelier, a few religious paintings—but the candles are new and alight. But by who? The man on the donkey? We are so alone up here; no-one has passed us on the road for the last few hours but someone has obviously been in here in the past fifteen minutes. We feel like intruders and go back outside, where long trestle tables and benches are stacked against the wall, evidence of the religious celebrations that go on up here.

Each church and monastery on the island is looked after by a family for a year—this is considered a big honour. Each church has its own naming day, a *pangriri*, when everyone walks to the church for a ceremony followed by eating, drinking and dancing that can continue until the morning. I find it hard to believe that the old people in the village could walk up here, but apparently they do, in a long procession. And a walk up here and a prayer in the church is supposed to make your loins more fertile. Truly. As my loins have long ago done their job and these things no longer interest me I find this a bit hard to believe, but apparently women who have trouble conceiving fall pregnant after just one visit up here. Stavros's wife told us this, and said that this peaceful place becomes a wild party venue at Easter, when everyone on the island makes the trip up to celebrate.

We wander around the outside of the monastery for an hour, just taking in the views. It is still and hazy, but we can look right down to the Port of Kamares in the distance—it looks tiny and without life. We get out our bread and cheese and make our modest picnic on the monastery walls and Geoffrey takes photos of our food, because he now regards himself as a food stylist as well as a top-class photographer. Our little lunch does not look encouraging, but it is a perfect memory of this day, this place, this moment.

'I would love to build a house up here,' I comment when we finish eating, letting my dreams run free. 'I'd like Balinese-style architecture with lots of bi-fold doors so the inside blends with the outside. And I want one of those wet edge pools that looks as if it melts into the sky and disappears over the mountain.'

Geoffrey says nothing for a long while, then says: 'I don't think Balinese would fit in with the Cyclades architecture here, and you'd need to build a funicular to get up and down the mountain, and that would cost millions.'

He can often stomp on my dreams.

After an hour it is time to head back and we leave, reluctantly. We are quiet on the journey down, Geoffrey eating his wild herbs, me still fantasising about my Balinese-style house. It is late afternoon and unbearably hot. Our faces and arms are sunburnt, and we are sweating and horribly uncomfortable.

It takes over an hour to get down, and when we do, we head for our private swimming hole by the rocks and jump in—fully clothed, with our hats still on. I won't bother telling you how good that felt; you can think about that yourselves.

After we have cooled off we wander back and see a sign that we had missed before (we aren't the most observant of people, as you have probably guessed by now). It points up the mountain and tells us it is eight kilometres to the top. So we have walked 16 kilometres today, half of it a tough uphill climb. I am a proud woman.

Later, on our veranda, gins and tonic sloshing in our bellies, Geoffrey with his nose in Wilbur Smith's latest, me back with Frances Mayes in *Bella Tuscany*, I come to the chapter where Francis leaves her beloved Tuscany for a visit to Sicily.

Her description and enjoyment of Palermo is so beyond beautiful I am gobsmacked. I cannot believe she and I had been in the same place: where I saw ugliness, she saw beauty.

'Listen to this,' I call to Geoffrey. 'Frances Mayes has been in Palermo five minutes and she's eating big risotto balls at the airport. I didn't see any risotto balls at the airport, did you?'

'Yes,' he replies. 'But I thought they were scotch eggs.'

I didn't see any of those either. I feel like someone posing as a travel writer who doesn't see the most obvious things in front of her. I read on.

'She's hasn't even left Palermo airport and yet writes about "a man with those amazing black, Sicilian, deep-as-wells eyes". Did you see any deep-as-wells eyes at the airport?' I ask.

'No, only my own bloodshot ones in the mirror in the men's room.'

'And she talks about "a parade of these intensely Italian-looking Italians. Women with gobs of dark curls cascading and flowing, slender men who seem to glide instead of walk." I didn't see any gobs of dark curls or gliding men. Did you? I saw just the usual rabble of scruffy, bored people you see in airports all over the world.'

There is a long silence from Geoffrey, and then: 'There was one very smart-looking woman sitting near us wearing tights which were cut off at the lower legs. She was very attractive.'

My dear darling Geoffrey is not one of those men who look at women in that sexually appraising way. He would never dream of ogling young gorgeous girls, even surreptitiously, because they would remind him too much of his own two lovely daughters.

'A woman with cut-off tights?' I cannot help but laugh at his inadequate description.

'Yes,' he says. And that is about all he can recall of this Palermo airport vamp.

I take a smug look over the top of my Frances Mayes book towards Geoffrey and then my view to the mountains and monastery, and think how reassuring it is to have a man who doesn't notice much detail on a gorgeous woman but can spot a wild rosemary bush 100 metres away.

It's impossible to keep track of the days but we have semblances of a routine now. Geoffrey zooms off on the scooter each morning and brings back warm bread and chocolate croissants, and then reads while I write for a couple of hours at the small table he has kindly pulled in front of the door of the living room. I am hopelessly romantic about this notion of writing in a foreign country while looking through a door (a delightful blue shuttered door in this case) to a magnificent view. I fancy myself as being here to complete the world's next best-seller, to bring my readers all the pleasures I am experiencing myself each day. But actually it isn't romantic at all. I sit on a narrow wicker chair in my underpants (I've taken up Geoffrey's habit of lolling about in underwear—it's very relaxing), and after fifteen minutes my sun-burnt legs stick to the chair and my back aches because I have spent far too many hours lying in bed, on the sand and on rocks.

And my gorgeous view is somewhat interrupted by Geoffrey sitting on a plastic chair—yes, in his underpants—just outside the door. Sorry, I shouldn't have spoilt the image for you, should I? But you need to know the truth.

Yesterday we spent the afternoon at our secret little cove and water-hole—we now know it has a name: Agia Marina—and although it is really just a pleasant stroll around the bay, it looks a long way from our villa. It is a tiny cove with large looming rocks that require much scrambling and cursing to traverse, and the little beach is just hard pebbles. It is the clear, deep water we love.

'How come we don't have such clear water at home in Australia?' I ask Geoffrey, because I am ignorant about such things.

'Because we have sand at the bottom of our oceans and it is stirred up by the waves,' he says. 'It makes it murky.' I don't know whether or not he's making this up but it sounds reasonable enough.

There is no sand on the bottom here, just rocks and pebbles, and although I am swimming in very deep water I can see right down to the bottom. It is so sensuous and thrilling that I make loud whooping noises, which startle the guests sitting on a small balcony in the villa above, but I don't care.

Night-time means a visit to the Captain's Bar, a trendy bar on the beach which would have a good vibe if only there were more people around. Although it is the height of summer, Sifnos is not thrumming with tourists. The Canadian girl who manages the bar tells us it will be a very different thing in August, when the place is jumping. At the moment it could only be described as limping, with just Geoffrey and me giving off an old-people vibe as we sit with our drinks and peanuts. Our bar manager plays rousing music to give the impression to everyone out on the street that it is all happening inside the Captain's Bar and quite a few people actually pop their heads in for a look, but they quickly remove them when they see just the flabby old couple in the corner. Tonight our manager is playing military marching music, and we order white wine and try to restrain ourselves from getting up and marching around the bar.

The bar is open to the beach and we spot our kind German father with his plump boys again. He walks along the beach with them, holding all their bulky beach gear and their hands at the same time, while the mother follows serenely behind.

This evening we wander over to the other side of the harbour; we want to try a new taverna and be able to look back over to our villa and the mountain beyond. We choose a place right on the water. The lights are starting to come on all over Kamares and it's very romantic.

Sifnos is renowned for its clay pot dishes, cooked for many hours to bring out flavours and make the meat melt in your mouth. We order lamb with red wine and chickpeas, which just tastes like the most ordinary stew with a can of chick peas thrown in it, and then we go for the house specialty of chickpea balls, little fried things that don't taste of much at all.

We have found all the Greek wait staff so efficient that they can have you served in minutes—we know this means the food has been sitting around in warming trays all day, but hey, it is fast. They bring out the cutlery in the breadbasket in one hand, and the water and wine in the other. The variety of wine containers keeps us interested every evening. Yes, I know a container means we are mean enough not to buy bottled wine and stick to the house wine, but what can I say? We *are* cheap. Tonight our wine container is a vivid pink aluminium thing with a long handle. We like it. And we like this fast service: a Greek waiter will have you seated, watered, wined and nibbling on a bit of hard bread within ninety seconds of entering his establishment. This is fact because I timed it one night and I wrote about it in my diary the next morning.

AN INVASION BY A
THOUSAND TOURISTS

'A thousand people will be coming to the island this weekend,' Stavros tells us proudly when we wander down to his hotel to borrow yet another book. 'It's a long weekend in Athens, and people will be getting out of the city.'

We are not sure if this is good or bad, but it might liven us up from our veranda lethargy, and a bit more action in the Captain's Bar would be fun. We decide a thousand extra people on the island will be agreeable, so long as we can remain aloof and hoity-toity up on our hill and join them only if we want to.

We have made many trips all over the island on our nifty red scooter, enjoying the stark landscape, discovering all the small languid bays, revelling in the knowledge that we have time to, well … revel. We have come to love the brown hills and stony fields, the smug feeling of being alone on the island once we leave each small village.

Today we drive right down to the water's edge at the small and pretty Vathy Bay, on the western side of the island. The bay is lined with tavernas spreading their tables out onto the sand, and is cut in two by a stately whitewashed church with a flat quadrangle of concrete reaching out over the water. We choose the most humble of all the simple tavernas beneath the tamarisk trees, where the table legs are sinking into the sand and the gingham tablecloths are covered with plastic.

One of the most pleasing aspects of Greek culture is the welcome you are given in these small places even if you spend just a euro or two. You can bring out your scrabble set and sit at a table in your swimmers for an entire afternoon for the price of a beer if you want to. We, of course, have no scrabble set, and enjoy far more than just a single beer. Barrels of wine and platters of food are more our style, so we settle our bums into the wicker chairs, make the legs sink further into the sand and feel as close to the water and contentment as is possible. Around the bay some of the new whitewashed houses and hotels have trails of purple bougainvillea growing up their walls, but not enough for my liking. A place as pretty as this should be covered in colourful vines, filled with pots of blooming flowers. I make a mental note to speak sternly to the Vathy Chamber of Commerce person about potting more geraniums and trailing more bougainvilleas.

We look at the menu: chickpea fried balls, tzatziki, Sifnos soft cheese, and salads of boiled grass and of string beans. The same as everywhere else, but here they also serve 'hourly' dishes, whatever they might be, and—even more puzzling—'kind' meat.

'Kid meat I think,' I finally say knowledgeably, but I don't order it. After looking fondly at the goats hobbling by our villa every night I could never bring myself to eat such a thing.

'How about "rabbit in origin"?' Geoffrey says. 'Or do you think they mean oregano?'

I do indeed think oregano, because there is enough of it growing wild on this island to flavour every clay pot in Europe.

We settle for the safety of a Greek salad and watch the beach action. An old man wanders onto the sand with a shopping trolley, and this keeps us happy until an enormously fat Englishman, sits—with difficulty—at a table behind us and starts chatting to a German couple nearby. It appears he lives permanently in Sifnos and owns a small hotel in Vathy Bay. He talks about the horrors of development, pointing to a sprawling hotel being built on the hill among the farms behind us.

'They'll be charging 500 euros a night for a room there,' he says in a broad northern English accent—500 euros is about the equivalent of $1000. As we are paying about the equivalent of $60 a night for an entire villa with stunning views in Kamares, I find this hard to believe. But this man knows. He's telling the polite German couple, who are trying to eat their Greek salads and drink their beers, that Vathy has gone to ruin; he's thinking of going back to England because things just aren't what they used to be. He can no longer bring his car down the little track right onto the beach the way he used to, and walking the 100 metres from his hotel is out of the question because of the many steel pins in his legs. (Nothing to do with the enormous gut, of course.)

'No-one in the village minds me bringing the car down to the beach, apart from one old bitch,' he tells the Germans, who murmur polite condolences but refrain from making any comment about said old bitch.

'There's one in every village,' the man laments. He has another beer and then talks about the tragedy he endured being married to his last wife for twelve awful years. The Germans nod politely and eat their Greek salads.

'I wonder what people would think of us if they eavesdropped on us?' I ask Geoffrey, and then lead him into a raunchy conversation to see if any ears turn to our table. I remind him of the time we were in Mykonos eight years ago and accidentally stumbled upon a beach at the bottom of tall cliffs frequented only by members of the nude gay community ...

We had innocently walked down the path to the small bay, planning to spend a lazy day in the beautiful little cove, only to find several hundred naked men enjoying being together. This intrigued me, but alarmed Geoffrey. Unsure of what to do, we found a square centimetre of space among the naked flesh and arranged our towels. All around us the men went about their business, which mostly involved oiling each other with sun lotion in a way Geoffrey was not comfortable with—especially the couple next to us, who took it turns to go on all fours while the other did the oiling.

'We have to leave,' Geoffrey finally said, and I reluctantly agreed.

'It's only right to leave these men alone,' he said. 'It is their place. We shouldn't be here.'

Which was fair, I suppose. There were a few women on the beach but they were naked and gay too, and even this didn't encourage Geoffrey to stay. So we walked up the steps in the cliffs and found quite possibly the most inviting open-air bar in the whole world. On the top of the cliff and with stunning views, it was a big and circular, and a flamboyant man in a sarong was serving white wine over generous slices of fresh peach in tall glasses.

'Can we at least sit here for a while?' I asked. 'Have a glass of this beautiful wine?'

And Geoffrey agreed. As we settled at the bar stools with our drinks and looked down to the bay and the oiled naked men, we realised that this was of course a gay bar. Soon men of all ages and shapes, wearing only the tiniest excuses for swimmers, joined us at the bar, gave each other open-mouthed kisses and flirted outrageously with the saronged guy behind the bar, until Geoffrey could bear it no longer and made us leave.

It wasn't just gay men who went naked on the beaches in Mykonos. Everyone—old, young, fat, skinny, waxed, unwaxed, wrinkly, droopy and (rarely) pert—seemed happy to strut around without a stitch on. It would not have been so bad if the beaches hadn't been so small and crowded. There was nowhere to put your eyes that didn't involve looking at places that usually don't see much sunlight. Lying on your stomach and burying your nose in a book was one solution, but a look up from your pages for a bit of a breather meant coming up to a sight that could quite well haunt you for years. Sitting up was not much better. Rolls of blubber, sprawled legs, dimply cellulite and hanging boobs confronted you (and that was just me and Geoffrey). Lying down and closing your eyes was the only solution. We did that a lot.

We sit up on our veranda, letting the still of the evening steal over us, and wait for the thousand people to arrive. The last couple hours before sunset are our favourite time, almost as seductive as the long and blazing sunset itself. The beach empties, the scooters stop, the cafés quieten, the whole town is at peace. The only sound comes from the small playground of a little school near the bay, where a group of energetic boys play basketball each night. Their cheerful yelps blend with those of the dogs that run at their heels, and float gently up to us on the quiet air. As the evening grows softer, the lights come on in the tavernas across the bay and on the yachts tied at the jetty. The sun starts to glow orange and turn the sea into molten gold. We go very quiet then as we slowly chart the sun's progress until it dips behind the hills and the horizon.

After dark this evening, taxis, buses and cars line up by the jetty, ready to receive the thousand people. Around 10 pm the enormous brightly lit ferry sails grandly into port, does an elegant swing around in the harbour so it can reverse into the dock, and lowers its massive ramp to send out cars, trucks, bikes, scooters and a thousand people. It is chaos and madness for the next hour. Up on the hill, we light our candles, make spaghetti with fresh tomato sauce, pour the wine and watch.

'If someone had told me I would get this much thrill just out of watching a ferryload of cars and trucks and people disembark, I would have said they were stupid,' I say, because sitting up here and watching all the frantic action is rather exciting. Later, after our spaghetti, we sit on the veranda wall with our legs dangling over the side and have a last splash of wine as the various vehicles move the people from the port off to other parts of the island.

First the big buses rumble by, then the taxis, then the scooters and finally the walkers, with their backpacks or suitcases. The road from the port is the only one out of town, so everyone must pass below by us. When the ferryload is about halfway up the road, another enormous ferry appears, lit up and twinkling on the horizon. It glides in and ties up alongside the first one.

'Not another thousand people!' Geoffrey says. 'This is too much excitement for one small island, not to mention for us.'

Yet more bedlam, as the port authorities—the local postcard seller and butcher by day, I think—blow their whistles importantly, shout at people to move on, direct cars and buses. It's quite marvellous.

'It's time for bed; you've had enough excitement for one evening,' Geoffrey says and he's right.

And by the time we have prepared ourselves to retire, the trucks, cars, people and ferries have gone and Kamares is all calm and peace again.

Geoffrey returns from his chocolate croissant mission next morning like an excited Greek housewife.

'The fresh fruit and vegetable truck has just arrived at the little supermarket,' he says breathlessly. 'There are dozens of Greek mammas buying zucchini flowers and the pick of the tomatoes and bananas.'

'Well, didn't you join them?'

'I tried to, but they wouldn't let me get near the boxes. And don't tell me you would go to the trouble of stuffing and frying a zucchini flower anyway. Would you?'

'No, but I would have eaten the pick of the tomatoes and bananas. Did you see the thousand people?'

'No. Apart from the old women it was fairly quiet, actually.'

I look at Geoffrey and think that it is the leathery men with their worry beads in the cafés that he should be joining. He looks more and more like them every day.

I suggest lunch back at Vathy to escape the thousand people. We visit a taverna recommended for its outstanding food and friendly service and find outstandingly awful food and hostile service. But it could have just been a bad day for the owners. We couldn't get any of the surly girls to serve us, so finally we went into the kitchen to look for ourselves, and being greedy people by nature, we ended up with cheese balls, stuffed tomatoes, a Greek salad, half a greasy chicken and a ratatouille. Despite the awfulness of it we ate the lot and then fell asleep on the beach looking much like a couple of Demis Roussos clones—before he went on a diet.

This evening we do run into the thousand people. They are all eating at our favourite taverna on the beach at Kamares. We are there at a table on the sand before they arrive, studying the menu, which features all the dishes we have encountered on every other menu, but gives us the usual giggle over the translations. We have fried 'cheack' pea balls tonight. A variation on the 'chic peas', and an improvement on the enticingly named fried 'chicken pea' balls we've come across at other places.

'There's a rice sauce here,' Geoffrey says, and we spend five frivolous minutes trying to work out what that might be—we finally decide it could mean just about anything.

The place fills to capacity quickly, and a flurried, bossy waitress shouts frantically back into the kitchen as she tries to take orders, clear tables and bring out yet more tables for a never-ending procession of new customers. Beneath the trees the tables spread closer and closer to the water's edge as staff—including mamma from the kitchen and papa from his position playing cards at a table near the door just outside the kitchen—help bring out more furniture to accommodate anxious bottoms.

The mangy cats are out en masse tonight; obviously the word has gone out on the cat-vine that a thousand extra people in town means plenty of fish heads and scraps beneath tables. Restless kids run from table to table, gorgeous young girls bounce in in groups of four and six, and old people stagger in on the arms of their families.

Tiny green bugs fall from the trees above us into our wine glasses, the lights around the harbour twinkle, and the moon is reflected on the still water of the bay. We shuck off our sandals and dig our toes into the warm sand.

Our bossy waitress appears to have just one other waiter to help her, a young man who literally runs out of the kitchen with trays of food and jugs of wine and jumps over children, chairs and the small wall just outside the restaurant door. The sand slows him down a little, but this man is fast. We order tzatziki (again) and moussaka (yet again) and lamb in the clay pot (yes, more) and chips (why?). We were told only yesterday that the Greeks cannot do chips and this place has not proved that wrong. Flat soggy things come out, single layered on a small white plate. If you have ever saved the remains of your fish and chip takeaway and then reheated them in the microwave the next day, you'll have an idea of what these chips are like. (And please don't tell me we are the only pathetic people who actually save their leftover fish and chips.)

We have noticed a group of four attractive people at other tavernas on other nights, and here they arrive again. One handsome man (with gobs of curls, actually, and a fabulous body) in the group appears not to be with the others mentally. He sits and stares into space, making no attempt to join in the conversation while his beautiful wife—with enviable slim shoulders and the loveliest jaw line I have ever seen—

runs her fingers along his bare arms and strokes his hand. He ignores her, stares up to the sky, around the restaurant and down at his plate while the others talk and try to include him. Only occasionally will he open his mouth to speak in their direction.

'He's rude,' I comment, still surreptitiously looking at him. 'Why does he bother to come out with them if he's not going to join in the conversation?'

'Leave him alone; he's probably deaf.'

He isn't. But I do leave him alone, and look out for our German father with the chubby boys. I haven't seen him for a couple of days and I miss him. However, there are other intriguing people to watch. A man at a table in front of us wearing white pants and a jaunty white panama hat digs his bare feet into the sand and lights up a fat cigar. A young attractive couple beside us tongue kiss passionately while they wait for the running waiter to take their order. A group of three women at the next table can't sit still for a minute: they get up, wander around, come back, get up again, go out the back, come back, make calls on their mobiles. They wear jackets tied around their waist even though it seems impossible that the hot weather will change or the temperature drop even a degree.

At a table behind us, a middle-aged woman with, we presume, her old mother spends the entire evening on her phone, ignoring her mother, who just sits and slowly eats. The woman holds the mobile to her ear with one hand, and has a cigarette in the other. She talks and waves her cigarette at the phone, and the minute she finishes her loud conversation she dials again and has another animated conversation. A large family group comes in, complete with a matriarch of colossal proportions. (Hey, who am I to talk!) Her bottom hangs spectacularly over the edges of her wicker seat and the chair's legs sink so deeply into the sand that her nose is practically at table height and everyone towers above her at the table. It is so comical I have to turn away, but no-one at her table seems to notice anything funny about it. The cats beneath the tables are delirious with excess, gorging on small fish heads and soggy chips. Our waiter runs impossibly faster, balancing plates and glasses on trays, weaving and leaping his way around people and over cats and kids. My moussaka is blisteringly hot on the outside, stone cold on the inside. The lamb in the clay pot is so overcooked that the meat has the texture of cardboard. I tell Geoffrey I want to gather up all the people in this restaurant, put them on a charter plane and take them back to Australia to show them what distinctive cuisine we have, what different and clever food combinations we can do.

'I wonder how they'd like their eggplant dip—served with oven-roasted tomatoes, dressed rocket leaves and warm Turkish bread and followed by seared Atlantic salmon topped with salsa verde on asparagus mash?' I ask.

'Don't compare.'

'I can't help myself. How do you think they'd like a dish of mussels in a white wine and tomato sauce?'

'You're being a bitch again.'

'I know. We're spoilt in Australia with our imaginative cuisine. We have so many choices, and so much variety, don't we? Such good produce.'

'Yes, but you can't sit at a table with your toes in the sand, so shut up and enjoy the atmosphere.'

I pick a couple of green bugs out of my oily moussaka, shoo off a cat, wave away a thick cloud of cigar smoke, have another look at my non-talking man, narrow my eyes at the woman on the phone, watch the wet tongues slither at the lovers' table, have another soggy chip, and feel blessed.

TWO LADIES IN SIFNOS

Waking up at leisure is a luxury we have become used to. No office to get to, no deadlines to meet, no chores to be done, just a slow awakening, a sluggish realisation that there is no need to struggle to full wakefulness. Then I sit up unhurriedly, asking Geoffrey (nicely) to get up and throw open the blue shutters so I can look out to the sun shining on my beloved mountain. These are all small pleasures I want to savour and remember. The morning cup of tea, the chocolate croissants, the paperbacks and the English newspapers on the bedside table … there is nothing more I want in the mornings in Greece.

I have finished a book called *My Life on a Plate* by India Knight, an English journalist. She's one of those rare writers who makes you laugh out loud. Fay Weldon has entertained me with her feminist wit and sharp humour, and now I am back with one of my darling serial killers gouging out a few eyes in *Eyes of Prey*, by John Sandford. No-one does serial killers as well as he does, in my opinion, although my all-time favourite, the liver-eating Hannibal Lecter will forever remain dear in my heart.

My pleasure in the English tabloids grows, even though we have to pay the equivalent of six dollars to buy the wretched things each day. I avidly follow Becks' controversial departure from Manchester to Real Madrid, despite never having sat through a game of soccer in my life. Of course it's his wife Posh's glamorous clothes and fake boobies that really interest me.

Posh and Becks are on the front cover of the papers every day, and so would you and I be if someone was willing to pay £30 million for the pleasure of having us in their club. If only we knew then that being on the front pages for being fabulous and wanted was the extent of the story—and how we gobbled up the juicy gossip much later back home when all those women leapt out of the woodwork to accuse Becks of being such a philanderer. I can't even imagine the field days the English tabloids enjoyed then.

But with all this lolling about in bed in the mornings comes an unwelcome visitor. Guilt. It visits on a daily basis. I ask it to leave in the rudest terms imaginable but it keeps sneaking back in. I should be working just a little, getting interviews for my mate's radio show back home. There is no shortage of suitable interviewees on the island. Stavros's wife is an agreeable young English lass from Yorkshire who came to Sifnos for a holiday, met Stavros, fell in love, married him and stayed, and has been here working with his family businesses for about eight years. She has an Australian friend, also married to a local Greek man and living on the island. Both are good interview subjects, and when next I venture down the hill to the hotel to borrow more books I make a date to interview them. I'm committed now. Guilt has gone for a little while.

Today we visit Kastro, on the east coast of the island. It is another pretty village of white houses and handsome churches, perched precariously on top of yet another brown hill. It's just a short drive from Kamares on our sexy red motor scooter, but the wind in my eyes makes them weep copiously. Geoffrey, as well as being the World's Best Packer and the World's Best Eater of Plants, is also the World's Best Innovator. He makes a little protective pad of tissues to go around the rim of my sunglasses to keep even the smallest of breezes away from my eyes. It is a practical invention and works quite well, but I doubt I have ever looked so nerdy in my life—it's even worse than thirty-eight years ago without my front tooth. The minute we arrive at Kastro I whip the tissues out and try to look reasonable again, but motor scooters and glamour do not go well for old(er) ladies.

Kastro's narrow streets are pedestrian only, so we park the bike at the bottom of the town and walk up. All I can say is, Kastro is one heck of a gorgeous little town. A mini Mykonos without the naked gay men (sadly).

Geoffrey stands up against a blue door in one of the houses; it is no more than five feet (1.5 metres) high.

'We could never live here,' he says towering a good foot above it, and just then it opens and out comes a small, bent-over woman; she is miniscule, old. We leap away and laugh at our big size and awkwardness. We love these moody back street labyrinths that lead to other moody streets with small surprises around every corner. We are about 200 metres above sea level, and every time we come to the end of a street we find small squares surrounded by low white walls overlooking the flat blue sea.

We come to a building site; it is a large new home in the middle of construction, and there are few things in life that Geoffrey and I enjoy more than a scramble over a building site. When we were building our own house in Australia, we spent a year mooching stealthily over building sites after dark, poking, pondering and pinching ideas (and deep apologies now to all those people we stole ideas from), and enjoyed every naughty minute of it.

There are no workers here on this hot day—actually, we rarely see Greek workers on any day—so we walk over planks and jump over cement bags and see that this house on the cliff face looks onto probably the best views on the island. We are looking at a picture we have seen on a hundred postcards in all the shops on the island. A thin peninsula pierces the vast blue sea, with a slim crazy-paved path leading to a white monastery at the end of the peninsula. The starkness of the white against the brilliance of the blue is almost blinding, and we put on our sunglasses and stand and stare for many minutes. We continue through the three levels of this Greek home, wondering who the lucky people who own it are, and stay a long time in the upstairs bedroom gaping at the views until we are interrupted by a couple of other nosy tourists and scurry out.

Back out in the debilitating heat we look down to a tiny bay where the water is so clear we can see right down to its deep depths. I don't think I have ever yearned for a swim more. A couple do lazy breast-strokes in the water, their pale legs kicking out like frogs' legs and … what's that? … their white bare bottoms clearly visible in the water.

We take another long, winding, crazy-paved path down to the rocks to get closer, and then take the path to the church. It is shut, so we content ourselves with wandering around the outside looking up at its pure white walls. But our attention keeps returning to the big flat rocks now just a few dozen metres below us—and to naked people, most of them sitting still and flat like sunning lizards, some getting up and showing all their bits for brief moments before they leap into the cool water. I just have to join them, get into that water.

'But if you jump off those rocks you won't be able to get back again,' Geoffrey says, and he's right. Without the aid of a ladder attached to one of the huge rocks—and in the absence of industrial hoisting equipment—there is no way I could scramble back up them.

'There's an old ladies' beach around the other side,' Geoffrey the Observant says. 'It's a small bay where you can walk into the water rather than leap off rocks.'

We wander away, looking yearningly back at the nude swimmers. A man in a small red fishing boat circles the bay, feeding out a sinuous line of yellow fishing net. He makes for a perfect postcard picture— and we do indeed snap off a couple of dozen shots of him.

So back up we climb to get over to the other side of the hill, and then we get lost in the lovely tight streets until haunting music calls us from a small bar, a place that looks like a platform in the sky. We follow the music inside, like sailors being called by the siren's song, and gasp yet again at the fabulous views on the other side of the bar, out over terraced hills to the sea.

We plonk our sweaty bodies and untidy bags on one of the cream banquettes lining the platform. Dark attractive men, all with gobs of curls, surround us. A particularly swarthy handsome man sits at the bar sipping a coffee and smoking—he's so over-endowed with gobs of dark curls that I can barely take my eyes off him. I can't see if he has deep-as-wells eyes because he wears mirrored sunglasses, but he definitely qualifies in the gob stakes. (Sorry, I forgot for a moment that we are in Greece, not Sicily, which is where the men have gobs and deep wells.) All the attractive men here are eating desserts in tall glass bowls, squishy creamy things, but we want booze, even though it is just two in the afternoon. We get a little dish of nuts with our wine and we revel yet again, this time in the feeling of being suspended in the sky. The distant hills are splattered with patches of green and dotted with white homes and the ubiquitous churches.

'You've forgotten about your swim on the old ladies' beach,' Geoffrey says as we near the bottom of our glass of white wine.

'Yes, but can we ask for more happiness than this?' I reply, because the poignant music, the white wine, the incredible views and the excess of gobs has mellowed me to a droopy condition.

But an hour later I can, and do, ask for more happiness. But only by way of a bit of foam rubber for my aching bones and straining neck. The old ladies' beach is pebbled and bloody uncomfortable.

Sometimes, you simply cannot have it all. I accept that.

Later that afternoon we drive to Chryssopigi, another picturesque bay with a church on a thin peninsula—as usual, this features on all the postcards. Our noses lead us to the beachfront, and ignoring another much-photographed church we head for the first taverna, where we find, to our surprise, hordes of people, all eating prodigious meals—at five-thirty in the afternoon. Had we researched the eating habits of the Greek people before we left, we would have realised that this is the mezze time, the time when ouzo and sardines and other treats are taken to tide you over till dinner, at around 10 pm. But these people don't appear to be eating simple snacks or holding back on the portion sizes; they are tucking into big plates of salads, and icy beers and ouzo and wine.

An attractive waiter with a slim waist and thick hair brings another table outside for us, puts it in the shade of a tree and gives us a dazzling smile, and even when we order just a beer and a coffee he treats us like honoured customers who have ordered hundreds of euros' worth of food and wine and are certain to give him a big tip.

There is 'lamp' with wine and dill on this menu, which endears the taverna to me even more, but the action all around us is far more amusing than idiosyncratic menu mistakes today. Right in front of us, frolicking on the beach, is a group of young deaf people. They are all healthy and attractive and they signal furiously to each other as they throw frisbees. One of them is topless, but her energetic young breasts attract not the slightest bit of interest from anyone in the café, so intent are they on eating their fish and Greek salads and drinking red wine from glass carafes. The topless girl wears a G-string bottom—she is quite lovely except for her sour expression. A small puppy, obviously owned by the taverna family, bounces onto the beach in front of her and she kicks it crossly away. I decide I do not like this deaf girl with the sour face and fabulous tits.

You wouldn't either.

One of the deaf people has a spear gun, and he seems to have caught something. The group look on, signalling intensely to each other. It is absolutely silent, but their animation and excitement is clear and contagious. We sip our drinks and watch them at play, attracting each other's attention if a back is turned by throwing a ball or frisbee at one another. I am sure Geoffrey is thinking that having a deaf wife could be a convenient thing, but he's not so crass as to say so.

We decide to come back to this pretty beach and lively café tomorrow. The menu is the most comprehensive we have come across so far, despite its lack of fish. We have been disappointed by the lack of fish on most menus; those that do have it charge about 40 euros for the smallest piece of fish, and 65 euros for lobster.

Geoffrey says Greece is all fished out, there are no big fish left in the seas. I don't know where he comes up with these theories, but certainly I haven't seen any big fish through the clear waters—and if they were there they would certainly be most visible.

We drive back, buy two beach mats at Stavros's sister's supermarket, two euros each, and wonder why we have denied ourselves the pleasure of the beach mat before. This tiny supermarket is crammed with every commodity you would need to run a household, perhaps a small business, for a few decades. There is nothing you can't buy here, from sewing materials to fresh cheeses to beach umbrellas. Its aisles are so tiny you have to suck in your breath and walk sideways down some of them. I love it.

We are complete failures as far as trying to say even the most simple of Greek words is concerned. 'Thank you', one of the first words even the most ignorant of tourists manages to learn in a foreign country, eludes us. It must be one of the hardest of all Greek words to say. *Efcharisto.*

Go on, try saying it clearly. Pronounced ef-cha-ree-sto. It doesn't seem so bad when you break it down, but although I study it in my guidebook each morning and say it aloud ten times before I go out, do you think I can say it to a waiter as he puts down a coffee in front of me? I can't even get my tongue around a simple hello. *Geiasas*—pronounced yes-as.

Sarah, Stavros's wife, speaks fluent Greek. She sounds super clever, babbling quickly into the phone, then switching to English with a strong Yorkshire accent when she looks at us. Sarah has lived on the island for eight years, and says the language was a complete blur to her for the first two years. She could not understand a single word being said around her, which in hindsight, she says, was a good thing—an English girl marrying a man born and bred in Sifnos with an extended family and a dozen potential wives lined up for him, had a lot to make up for. She is glad that she had no knowledge of what was being said about her in those first two years of marriage. Now that she has given Stavros and his family three gorgeous children and can cook moussaka, she is well and truly one of them, and she loves her Greek family. Stavros not only owns two hotels, a villa or two, apartments and other prime real estate; he is also a goat farmer, a chicken keeper, an olive oil maker and a winemaker. He never stops working. Every year when he and Sarah go to England for their Christmas break, he buys a bit of farming or hotel equipment.

This morning I interview Sarah and her friend Lynne in the small café opposite Stavros's hotel while a neighbour in the gift shop keeps an eye on the reception desk for Sarah. As a funky young waiter with thickly gelled hair serves us orange juice, I ask Sarah about the seasonal changes in life on a Greek island.

'January and February are the quietest months,' she says. 'People take this time to slowly do repairs to their hotels and shops from the previous summer season and get ready for Greek Easter, which could be in March or April. After Easter, the tourist season starts, and it runs until October. We do grape picking in September, olive picking in

November and then we go walking around the mountains while we prepare for Christmas at home in England.'

'That's wonderful,' I screech and pull back the microphone before she has actually finished speaking.

'Yes, I love it here now, but it did take a lot of adjusting in the beginning. Actually it was quite tough.'

'That's wonderful.'

'I did miss my family in England an awful lot.'

'That's wonderful.'

'And I don't think Stavros's family really liked me in the beginning.'

'Oh, that's just wonderful.'

Sarah then changes the subject to olive oil, which I also think is just wonderful, and tells me that she and Stavros make about 100 litres a year, enough for themselves and Stavros's mother for a year.

'We make our own wine as well,' she says.

'That's wonderful.'

'Stavros stomps the grapes himself.'

'How wonderful.'

'It gets very cold here in the winter.'

'Wonderful.'

And that ends our interview. Sarah looks most relieved.

I turn to Lynne, who looks a bit pale around the gills—I can't think why—but she is brave.

'Where in Australia do you come from, Lynne?'

'Canberra.'

'Wonderful. Was it a big culture shock? I mean, Canberra is a bit different from a small Greek island, isn't it?' (You can't say I don't ask meaningful questions.)

'Yes. Very.'

'That's wonderful.' (Or give meaningful responses.)

'I adjusted very slowly,' she says carefully. 'I speak fluent Greek now, but I don't think I will ever be Greek. It's such a different culture. I've been here for sixteen years now, but I still think of myself as Australian.

You never lose what you had in your childhood. I still love to come across any kind of product from my childhood, because it makes me feel connected. Even Fairy Washing Liquid gives me a thrill because it is what my mother used when I grew up. You will always be homesick for those childhood memories. You will always have that feeling. We are accepted here, but only as foreigners. But even people from Athens are regarded as foreigners by the Sifnos people, so that's okay. Even people in the capital, Apollonia, regard us here in Kamares, a mere five kilometres away, as foreigners.'

'That's wonderful. Do you get bored in the winter months?'

'No. Most people here have more than one job. Their summer business is not enough to support them, so almost everybody grows vegetables, has goats, sheep, and chickens. We grow vegetables for our own household, but now we are finding we cannot grow enough for a whole year. We grow onions and plait them to put down for the following year. I've plaited a lot of onions in my time here, but we find now that we run out before the year is up. My husband's parents own a hotel which has its own restaurant, his brother owns a hardware shop, his sister has a patisserie, and another brother owns a cheese shop.'

'That is especially wonderful. How come a girl from Canberra came to Sifnos?'

'I was travelling, doing the Europe thing, and I came here because a travel guide told me Sifnos was a small, quiet island and I liked the sound of that. I stayed at my future husband's family hotel and had breakfast, lunch and dinner there every day, and I knew I was going to say goodbye to Canberra.'

'How wonderful.'

'My children were born on the island, even though there is no hospital on the island and there is always a risk.'

'How positively wonderful.'

'Fortunately, everyone was okay.'

'How sad.'

'Sad?'

'Sorry, I was just becoming horribly aware of how often I say "wonderful".'

Lynne is sweet. She hides her amusement well and refrains from telling me I am a far from wonderful interviewer. She ploughs on.

'There is a tremendous community spirit on the island. It's very safe here. I never lock my car or house. I leave the key in the motor scooter. If things are lost or left behind anywhere they are always taken to the police station for collection.'

'Wonderful. Wonderful. Wonderful. Do you ever have anyone famous visit the island?'

'Oh, yes. Many celebrities. Most of them stay on their own yachts, which they anchor outside the bay so that they are not hassled by tourists. Mel Gibson and his family were in the ice-cream shop here one day. They looked so like any other family that I didn't realise who they were. The kids were harassing Mel for ice-creams and he was reacting just like any harassed father, urging his kids to hurry up and choose a flavour.'

'That's pretty wonderful.'

'Rod Stewart wandered into the foyer of our hotel in a sarong to choose a book from the bookshelves,' Sarah says. 'And George Bush snr and his wife sailed in, in a most lavish yacht. I think George Bush jnr was with them too. But it was a while ago. The Greek Prime Minister comes to Sifnos often. He's a most unpretentious man; he sits in the waterfront cafés without bodyguards and enjoys a coffee. Robert Mitchum used to come. The Crown Prince of Denmark came once but nobody knew who he was so it didn't cause any excitement, until a Danish couple arrived and almost went crazy. They followed him all over the island.'

The three of us look out across the blue bay thinking about rich people and Rod Stewart in a sarong, and I ask Sarah if she knows who owns the house that Geoffrey and I trespassed on the day we first arrived.

'A woman skin specialist from Athens,' she says. 'She just uses it for the summer. Norman Mailer's ex-wife comes to visit her and so does Camilla Parker-Bowles.'

'Wonderful.'

Then we all look up to the top of the brown hills.

'Why do you have so many churches on the island, why build more all the time?' I ask ignorantly.

'A pledge, a thank you to their religion,' Sarah says.

I tell her the monastery up on the hill had its candles burning when we walked up there, even though we had seen no-one apart from the donkey man on our walk up there.

'People will call in and light candles as they pass. Even someone tending his goats or chickens will light candles. It is something everyone does,' she says.

And when you think about it, if you live in a community where you can leave your house and car unlocked, ask your neighbour to mind your hotel while you go off for a coffee, make a year's worth of olive oil for your mother-in-law, and have the goat herder light candles in your church, there is not much else to say about it, other than it's bloody well spit-in-your-eye wonderful. Isn't it?

SAD FAREWELLS

The time has come to leave Sifnos and we feel heavy in the heart, which makes a pleasant change from feeling heavy in the stomach. We leave tomorrow, but it is not all sadness: we're only going as far as Athens, where we are boarding a tall clipper ship for a week of indulgent cruising around Greece and Turkey.

Sifnos has worked its way right into my psyche with its charismatic bays, white churches, clear water, small fishing villages, rolling hills and friendly people. Geoffrey agrees, and says we should milk the next twenty-four hours for all we can. We spread out our now well-worn map of Sifnos on the table and pore over it to see if there is any little bay, remote village or tall mountain we haven't visited yet. And there is one bay we have not yet visited—it's called Cheronisos, and it's right at the very top of the island.

We stop on the way in Apollonia to buy sunscreen, and inside a dark and musty shop, which looks much like a chemist masquerading as a haberdashery trying to be a grocery store, I run into Lynne, who is buying tape to mend the curtains in her family's hotel. She is loud with excitement because she's seen a copy of the *Australian Women's Weekly Cookbook* in the shop.

'Can you believe this!' she says, holding the book, flapping it in front of the face of the shop's owner. 'The *Women's Weekly Cookbook*—I love it!' Lynne's affection for all icons Australian makes no impression on the Greek women, so we wander outside and I listen until Lynne calms down about the *Women's Weekly*. I try to understand her excitement, go along with her enthusiasm, but I just can't. Mind you, I haven't lived on a tiny Greek Island for sixteen years tending goats and plaiting onions.

We ride north until the road runs out at the top of the island and we are on a thin and desolate peninsula, a narrow bit of a bone-jarring unmade road. I clutch onto Geoffrey's ever-growing love handles and become nervous about being so far from humanity. I ask him to turn back.

'No, we've come this far, we are not turning back now,' he says.

It feels completely isolated, as though we have driven into an uninhabited land. We look down the cliffs on either side to the blue ocean, and although it is quite spectacular, I don't like it. Just when I am about to exert my will as well as my grip on Geoffrey's love handles, he starts to go down a rocky track, and the feeling of being in wild outback country grows more intense. Then suddenly we round a tight corner and come across a cheerful sign advertising Cornetto ice-creams. Well, like a soul lost for weeks in the desert without sustenance or sight of mankind, I am overjoyed at the thought of being offered a chocolate-coated Cornetto. The Cornetto sign is attached to a small white building, the local store, which leads us on to perhaps the most pretty of all the fishing villages we have encountered yet.

'And you wanted to turn back,' Geoffrey says as we park the scooter. We step over piles of bright yellow fishing nets on the jetty and look at the colourful wooden boats dotting the bay and the whitewashed houses clustered on the surrounding hills.

As we plonk ourselves down on the warm sandy beach we hear American voices all around us, and I wonder how they knew about this place when we didn't.

I so love these tiny places where the boats and fishing nets are not just scenery, because the locals really do continue their uncomplicated routines around the tourists. Tiny tavernas line the small sheltered bay and spill onto the sand, and we feel confident of a warm welcome whether we want a multi-course extravaganza or just a bottle of water.

We pass up the 'burning pepper plant salad' and order yet another Greek salad, some fried squid and half a litre of wine served in what looks like a bailing cup. (You know, for bailing water out of leaking boats.)

It is so idyllic and undemanding here, so relaxed and casual, that I could weep at the thought of leaving it all behind tomorrow. Instead I ask Geoffrey if it wouldn't be too greedy to order another bailing cup of wine. He agrees with alacrity—he's probably been having similar thoughts. We watch the people on the beach, just a metre directly in front of us, especially the American man who is brushing every bit of sand from his feet, doing a seesaw thing with his socks between his toes to remove every grain (who wears socks on a Greek island in summer anyway?) and we eavesdrop on their conversations, which are typical of most American travellers—they are amazed that they can't order mustard with their meat and mayo with their fries, and are thoroughly confused by the oil and vinegar put on the table with their Greek salads. Later, I swim for an hour in the clean warm water, doing an old-fashioned dog paddle past the fishing boats and out of the bay, looking up the tall rock faces to the white buildings and down to the tiny fish brushing my legs. It is a most sensual experience, but it all disappears instantly when I emerge from the water to find Geoffrey on his side in the sand snoring. Apart from that, it is a day where we have made more beautiful memories.

While we sit near to tears on our veranda on our last evening, we see an elegant sailing ship anchored in the harbour. It looks very much like the one we are to board tomorrow. Its sails are down, but with its stately white hull and tall masts it still cuts a romantic figure in the bay just before sunset.

'It must be the *Star Flyer*,' I say even though we can't see its name, and immediately feel a little better about leaving in the morning. It finally sets sail, bound for Athens to await us, we hope, and we sit for a long time, silent and thoughtful as it makes its graceful way towards the horizon and the sunset. We cruised on *Star Flyer* last year, but there are a number of these sailing ships on the cruise circuit now and it is impossible to know if this is our ship.

'It doesn't get much more romantic than that,' Geoffrey says and then burps lustily.

Later we go down to the harbour front for one last meal in our beloved Kamares. For a change, we choose one of the two Italian restaurants. We have watched these two Italian restaurants every evening as we have passed on our way to other harbourside frivolity. One has remained empty night after night; the other has thumped with activity. We have seen this same situation in our hometown in Australia: two restaurants, side by side, serving equally good food and wine, giving equally good service, one struggling to fill two tables a night, the other vibrating with activity. Here in Sifnos, we feel sorry for the lonely one, but choose the lively one, which is why the lonely one is doomed forever to be lonely and the lively one will prosper—no-one wants to be the loser sitting in an empty restaurant.

Our table is right on the roadside, and I mean that literally. My toes are in danger of being run over by a passing scooter, so I keep them under the table. I order spaghetti napolitana and Geoffrey orders a stuffed pizza, having no idea what it is. We actually sit through three ferryloads of busy disembarkation while we eat, which is more entertainment that you could expect to find at a Broadway show.

'It is awesome when the ferry disembarks' I have written in my notes. 'The harbour fills with noise and flurry. Huge refrigerated trucks bear down on us in the narrow street, almost lopping off my toes.'

What more thrills could you ask for with your stuffed pizza?

The restaurant is across the road from the Captain's Bar, and as usual, it has no customers. I mentally urge some of the passers-by to stop for a drink and liven the place up, but no, it remains quiet. We people-watch for a couple of hours from our excellent vantage point. It seems the Greeks are almost as fervent as the Italians when it comes to evening strolling. Every local has donned their Sunday best and is out strolling this evening. Smartly dressed mothers holding hands with attractive young fathers push wide-eyed babies in prams. One old couple strolls along, his arm slung protectively around her shoulder; she is bent almost double with osteoporosis. They go from one end of the harbour to the other and it takes them about an hour. We watch a white-haired old woman sitting in front of her apartment across the street on a strip of footpath no wider than her chair. Her toes dangle onto the road. Behind her, the doors to her modest apartment are open—a shabby wardrobe and a single bed are all the furnishings to be seen in the small room—and I feel as though I am looking right into her life.

'What a pity that old woman has to live in such small quarters with so little furniture,' I say to Geoffrey in between mouthfuls of spaghetti.

'Don't be silly,' he says. He looks frightened of his stuffed pizza—it's a big pouch of pastry and he isn't too sure if he wants to cut into it. 'She is on the beach side of the road. She has the beautiful bay and beach to look at from her windows on the other side. She probably owns all the buildings along the front and is collecting big rent, especially from the empty Captain's Bar next door.'

He's right. I judge people and situations too quickly and always on face value.

In the morning, after we have checked out with Sarah at the Hotel Stavros and are waiting for the ferry to take us to Athens to meet the

Star Flyer, Stavros runs up to us in the queue, says he's been too busy with his goats and grapes and he's sorry he almost missed us. He hands us a bottle of his own yellow olive oil and says he will await us on our visit next summer.

I sniffle all the way on the ferry to Athens.

A kind-faced young security man at the port in Athens sees something suspicious in our hand luggage as it passes through the X-ray machine and asks, apologetically, if he can examine our bag. I think it must be all the wires and bits of equipment for my tape recorder, and I feel sorry for the poor man as he pulls on thin rubber gloves. He's going to need them. There are unwashed underpants in there, a revolting toilet bag full of greasy, half-used products, a bottle of gin, and countless boxes of pills and potions of the kind required by middle-aged people when they travel. Heartburn medicine, indigestion tablets, high blood pressure medication, and hormone tablets are squeezed into pockets and nooks in our bags. The young man tries to keep his expression bland as he picks his way through all this horrible stuff but he can't help but wrinkle his nose as he transfers a packet of gum massaging sticks to the pocket with the bottle of digestive cleanser and the packet of senna tablets. He looks suspiciously at the tape recorder with a jangle of wires hanging from it and I'm tempted to invite him to listen to it, but I don't want to repulse him further by making him listen to my 'wonderfuls', so I keep quiet. Finally he finds the doubtful product. It's Stavros's bottle of olive oil.

'What is it?' he asks, unscrewing the lid. I am tempted to tease him and say, 'A urine sample', but the man has suffered enough, so I tell him it is home-produced olive oil from Sifnos. This delights him, because he is from Sifnos himself and knows that its olive oil is the best in the world. We all grin like idiots and take turns to sniff the good olive oil, keeping our eyes averted from the gin bottle and pills bursting from the bag.

'I can't think of many jobs more horrible than his,' Geoffrey says as he stuffs unwashed undies and gin back into the bag.

The *Star Flyer* is a replica of the stylish old sailing ships that used to grace the waters in the late nineteenth century. It is owned by a wealthy Swedish man who had the romantic notion to duplicate the beautiful tall ships, but fit them out like millionaires' yachts so people could enjoy an authentic old-fashioned sailing experience with all modern conveniences. We discovered this type of cruising through a friend, and fell madly in love with the whole sailing experience on *Star Flyer* when we cruised around the Italian and French Rivieras a couple of years ago.

'It's about cruising in the traditional way,' we were told by the enthusiastic travel agent when we first went. 'You can take part in hoisting the sails if you want to or just watch as the ship sails into the sunset every evening. It's very romantic.'

There'll be no sail hoisting for me this time. I intend to lounge by the pool, sink into one of the comfortable chairs in the oak-panelled library, and sit at the Tropical Bar on the back deck drinking champagne and making new friends.

And drink champagne is what we do the minute we step on board, because there is a beaming Filipino barman called Ramon waiting there with a glass, and the most beautiful white-toothed smile I've ever seen.

Perhaps the most pleasing thing about *Star Flyer* is that it takes only about 120 passengers. And there is none of that big cruise liner mentality either. No bingo allowed here. No Las Vegas-style shows either. Nor is there specified seating for dinner, which means that if you take an instant dislike to someone on the first night you can dodge them at dinner for the next seven days. Which is what I intend to do after sitting with an Australian couple from outback Queensland last night. Nothing wrong with Queenslanders; I am one myself now. It's just that this couple is too Aussie for me. He uses expressions such as 'flat out like a lizard drinking', and she is too loud and confident and asks too many questions—can talk under wet cement with a mouth full of marbles, in other words. He announces to the table that he is—and fair dinkum proud of it—a scrap metal merchant. They have been in Europe to attend an international scrap metal merchants' conference (yes, I can hardly believe it myself) and are having a break after the stress and pressure of the seminar.

Perhaps ... if I am truthful ... I don't like them because they take the attention away from me. Being used, these past months, to continental people and American tourists getting excited about my Australian accent, I am probably jealous because they have stronger accents and everybody else at the table is eager to listen to them talking about the intricacies of the scrap metal business while stoning the crows and drowning the dingoes. There, I've been honest. I feel better now.

We spend the next day at sea, watching the Captain on his bridge and the crew hoisting ropes and doing other nautical things while we laze around on the decks sussing out all the other passengers.

Now, you don't know this about me, because I haven't told you yet, but I am an honorary ex-merchant sailor. I have spent many years at sea, often for nine months at a time, sailing on huge ocean liners, multi-storey oil tankers and creaky old cargo ships. It was all thanks to Geoffrey, who was an engineering officer when I met him on board an ocean liner sailing from Southampton to Australia in the mid-1960s. There he was at the Captain's cocktail party, giving sherry to an old lady: white jacket, gold braided epaulettes, lots of fluffy curly hair and big thick horn-rimmed glasses.

'Who's that?' I asked a young officer I had quickly befriended.

'It's big Geoffrey,' the guy said.

'I want to meet him,' I told the guy. Being a very tall woman, I always sought tall men across crowded rooms. In the 1960s short men would never approach a tall woman—now they don't seem to have a problem, thank heavens—and who knows how many short men in the past missed out on the pleasure of me because of it?

Anyway, the guy called Geoffrey over and introduced us with an 'Ann would like to meet you' line, whereupon the gallant Geoffrey looked me up and down and said, 'That's because I'm the only man in the room bigger than you.'

His first words to me. All the more stinging because they were true.

I won't bore you with unwanted details of our shipboard romance other than to say I fell madly in love with him over the next five weeks, and by the time the ship docked in Australia I knew I wanted to marry him, which I did a few months later, when he came sailing back to Australia. And then off I sailed into the sunset with him—wives were allowed to, and wanted to, travel with their seafaring husbands in those days.

For the next ten years we stationed ourselves in Southampton in the UK and did trips all over the world on different ships. We sailed from England to the Persian Gulf around the Cape of Good Hope a hundred times to bring oil back from Dubai. We brought coal back to England from Japan and apples and lamb from New Zealand and coconut oil from the Philippines. The ships would stay in port for weeks sometimes to load cargo, which meant we had a chance to explore many exotic countries and experience life that most young people our age could only have dreamt of.

Of course I recorded nothing of our adventures back then. A well-written detailed dairy would have been an invaluable thing to look back on now, nearly forty years later, but there are only a few old small photos to bring back the memories. There was usually only one other female, sometimes two, on board, and I lived with seventy men quite happily. There were boring times, of course—hundreds of long hours to fill at sea, especially when we travelled the Pacific towards Australia;

the clocks were put back an hour every day and the evenings felt as though they would never end. I used to knit a lot (good heavens, did I really?). On one long trip I knitted a coat. Yes, a coat. It was a three-quarter length coat in orange, brown and yellow wool with big loops all around the bottom and around the sleeves, if you can imagine such a hideous thing. As the knitting grew, I became so involved I wouldn't go ashore on excursions.

'No, I've got ten more rows to finish on the sleeve,' I said one day as a dozen of the off-duty officers made plans to go on a trip up a river on one of the islands in the Philippines.

'Come on, come with us,' Geoffrey urged, but I was nearing the end of a sleeve, and I just couldn't leave my knitting at such a crucial point.

So off they all went and I spent the afternoon in my small dark cabin, finishing my sleeve and making a thoroughly good start on the next one. I was thrilled with my progress when they returned to the ship later that day—until they told me of most amazing adventures rafting up the river to small towns where they watched the locals making wood carvings and found funky little bars and restaurants and ate with more locals and rode in cute little tuk tuk machines. They were over-joyed with their experiences, and these were men used to foreign and unusual places.

And I had sat in my dark cabin knitting all afternoon.

To this day, I still don't see an opportunity, even when it stands up and bites me.

And I looked like a big giraffe in that coat.

A BIT OF LUXURY

Did I say the best thing about *Star Flyer* was the relaxed dining arrangements? Or was it the lack of bingo? It's neither. It's the Swedish sports team; two beautiful young blonde men. I can't stop looking at them. What is it about Swedish people? So healthy, glowing, beautiful. Is there an ugly person in Sweden? If you've seen one, I'd like to know, please.

Last night we were treated to a concert put on by the crew. It seems you have to be able to sing like Frank Sinatra as well as make a great martini if you want a job as barman on *Star Flyer*, because Ramon, our beaming Filipino barman, was the star of the concert with his sexy version of 'My Way'. And it is not enough to be a handsome qualified diver and speedboat driver if you want a job on the sports team on *Star Flyer*; you also have to be able to dance. Those two fabulous guys from the Swedish sports team did a raunchy mock strip. They took off their shirts, leapt up onto the bar and swung around a pole while all the old women perked up considerably—especially me. All the other crew members, from the deck hands to the officers, had some sort of talent, and they put on a really good show, from dance routines to guitar playing to sea shanty singing. I know it sounds corny, but I assure you it wasn't.

At lunch today we spy the scrap metal merchants talking animatedly to a table full of Americans, so we run down the other end of the dining room and sit with a gay couple from Brussels. One is a travel agent and the other has a back problem that prevents him from working in his normal job of supermarket layout person. They love the excuse to talk to us, to use their English. They talk about the changing face of Europe, how the influx of refugees from Russia, Bulgaria, Africa, Afghanistan and North Africa is completely changing most of Europe, its look, its culture, its economy, its religion, its values.

'There are pockets of refugees everywhere, and most of them do not assimilate into their new societies; they stay in their own groups and create their own cultures,' one of the Belgian guys says. 'Europe is not the same any more. Traditions and old European families will soon be all gone. We were travelling in Provence recently and were shocked by the lack of restoration of icons, and the shambles Provence is now because it is full of people who just do not care about preserving the heritage.'

Their dismay is so infectious that Geoffrey and I cannot think of a thing to say. We all go quiet and think about Europe not being Europe any more, and I feel a sudden stab of sadness because Europe features so importantly in my fondest memories of earlier travels. It almost brings a tear to the eye, so I go up to the Tropical Bar and have Ramon open a fresh bottle of champagne for me and look out to Rhodes as we approach. I did tell you I can sometimes be shallow.

Rhodes is the capital of the Dodecanese, a large island that is an important regional centre as well as one of the most popular of the Greek islands. It is also known as the island of sun, which explains why so many English tourists love it. It was part of both the Roman and Byzantine empires, before being conquered by the Knights of St John (yes, them again). They occupied Rhodes from 1306 to 1522, and their medieval walled city still dominates the town. The modern town of Rhodes has a cosmopolitan character and a lusty nightlife should we be fit enough to seek it, but we decide that once we have completed our tour, we are going to explore the medieval town, which is still surrounded by the high walls erected by those peripatetic knights.

We have booked the shore excursion of Rhodes even though we hate tours because we are afraid we are going to be surrounded by old people. Tours are always full of old people—you see them peering out of buses in every big city all over the world—and we are not quite ready to be as they are yet.

Our guide is chatty and informative as we drive away from Mandraki Harbour to Lindos, where we are promised an acropolis of jaw-dropping beauty. But before we get there we pass ugly high-rise buildings that do not in any way represent Greek architecture. This part of Rhodes is like a small city, complete with ugly office buildings, shops and a football ground.

'The population of Rhodes swells by one and a half million in the summer,' the guide says. That means a lot of tourist money coming to town.

'See that football ground,' he says. 'Hardly used. Greeks are not so stupid as to chase a ball around in the heat; they much prefer to sit in cafés drinking strong Greek coffee and playing backgammon.'

We pass an eighteen-hole golf course in a luxurious new resort development.

'Only used by tourists,' our guide says. 'Greeks are not so stupid as to chase a little white ball around. We prefer to sit in the cafés talking.'

We continue on past houses of the more typical Greek whitewashed architecture, but all, without exception, are unfinished. We have seen this everywhere in Greece. Homes occupied, and obviously not new, but with dangerous-looking reinforcing wires sticking up out of the roof.

'Greeks are not so stupid as to finish their houses,' our guide says. 'They have to pay tax when the house is finished so they never finish.

And Greeks are not so stupid as to not look after their families, so they leave the houses like this so they can build another storey for the children when they marry or for the parents when they are too old to care for themselves.'

Not so stupid at all, these Greeks. Saving taxes is everybody's business, even if it means living your entire life with big hunks of wire sticking out of your roof.

Well, the acropolis at Lindos is bloody fantastic. As our guide had told us, everyone thinks of Athens when they think acropolis, but this one on Rhodes is very famous, very old, and right now, very hot. We have walked up the hill while others chose to ride donkeys, and we have mistakenly taken the donkey path instead of the walking path, and therefore have followed donkey bums all the way up. We now smell, as well as being hot and extremely bothered.

The acropolis sits on a sheer precipice 125 metres above the village, and its columns are fabulously dramatic against the blue sky. It overlooks the brilliant blue sea, and the precipice splits two crescent beaches way below. The views are simply stunning, but there is no shade at all up here, and our guide tries to give as much information as quickly as possible. He talks of dates (Lindos was first inhabited in 3000 BC) and those damn Knights of St John again, and other interesting history, but it is hard to take anything in when standing bareheaded in 40+°C heat.

Tales of Greek gods blend with stories of knights and myths of Greek origin and facts about the Italians pinching most of the stuff from the acropolis when they occupied Rhodes from 1932 to 1943 ... it all goes in and then goes immediately out of our hot heads. We climb more steps and catch our breath at another stunning view as we come up to look over at the Temple of Lindian Athena, built in the fourth century.

'The Greeks are continuing the restoration of this acropolis but they aren't so stupid as to hurry,' the guide says. 'They do a bit of work in the morning, but when it becomes too hot they stop and come down for coffee. Everything must be done on Greek time. The same goes for the Olympics. If the work doesn't get done on time, we will have another opportunity for the Olympics another time.'

We leave the guide and wander by ourselves over the acropolis ruins and up the old steps, and peer between the graceful columns out over the clear blue sea and way down to the depths of the ocean floor. This water in the Aegean and Mediterranean is special; it makes you want to leap from great heights into its cooling depths. We stay for as long as we can bear the heat and then walk back down the proper walking path, which is lined with souvenir shops and local women selling the exquisite lace for which Lindos is renowned. But no-one buys any. We get down to the village and explore the narrow cobbled streets with the other tourists, and although it's busy with tourists the feeling is one of great personality. We peer through doorways into flower-filled courtyards, and into inviting cafés but—typical us—we have forgotten to bring money.

'It's because it is cashless on board the ship,' Geoffrey says, but that somehow doesn't seem to wash, because all the other passengers on the tour have wallets and purses and are buying bottles of water, postcards and beads.

Finally Geoffrey borrows some money from one of the passengers— I can't recall ever guzzling a whole bottle of water with such pleasure.

We go back to the ship, retrieve our wallets, and go forth to explore the marvellous streets of the old town. This part has been inhabited for more than 2400 years. A city was first built here in 408 BC and when those busy Knights of St John arrived in 1309 they built their citadel over these ancient remains. There is something quite thrilling about walking through gates in medieval walls, and this old town—now a world heritage site—has four kilometres of walls and eleven gates. We walk down the Street of Knights, past the palace of the Grand Masters and around to the Mosque of Suleiman. We resist all the spruikers in the colourful shops and cafés, and wander back to the area around St John's Gate, where we came in. A large fountain dominates the square, and all around us are shops and endless cafés. Suddenly it seems as though every café owner in the busy square knows us. They call out to us, wave, and invite us in.

'Do we know these people?' I ask Geoffrey. Even the waiters in the cafés upstairs in the surrounding buildings are hanging out of windows, signalling frantically and urging us to join them.

'Come on up,' a waiter in a bright red shirt calls from a window upstairs, as though he is a kind uncle welcoming us back after a lengthy absence.

'Come in, come in,' four waiters call in unison from an extended café crammed with tables and chairs and overlooking the fountain.

'I could go a beer,' Geoffrey says. I feel like a cool drink too, so we walk towards the four waiters at what appears to be one long café. A fight almost breaks out as they all grab at our arms, urging us to sit in their cafés.

'Isn't this one and the same place?' I ask as one man pulls out a chair, another moves a table, another yanks me towards another table and a fourth steers Geoffrey's bottom into an awaiting chair.

We have never felt so wanted.

'No, they are four different places,' one of the men says. 'And his is no good, so choose mine.'

Which prompts us immediately to choose another.

It seems ridiculous to be so competitive over something as small as the sale of a few drinks, but their competitiveness is fierce, unpleasant, and not exactly conducive to relaxing and drinking beer.

We finally choose a table in the middle café and while our waiter claps his hands with glee, the others stomp off huffily. They immediately perk up when another couple comes within range.

'Is it always like this, so competitive?' I ask our waiter when he brings a beer in an enormous glass boot and a glass of mineral water.

'Yes, always,' he says. 'I have to fight for every customer. It is all the fault of Bush. The war. Not enough tourists.'

We sip our drinks and watch the waiters argue over every person who wanders past and is silly enough to look in the direction of the cafés. At one point the arguing over an American couple is so heated that pushing begins.

'Do the right thing; I saw you first,' a particularly aggressive waiter says with outstretched hands to the couple, who only want a coffee or a beer and are now being confronted with a moral dilemma.

'You looked at my café first,' the waiter continues, and gives another waiter a sneaky push.

Finally the couple choose the café at the far end, and more waiter sulking ensues.

'Bush has a lot to answer for,' Geoffrey says and orders another beer in a glass boot.

A couple we have noticed on the ship wanders into the square, looks over at the cafés and the whole performance starts again. They are coerced into our café and sit at a table right next to us. Once the fighting has stopped we chat. They are from Brazil. She is dark and petite, with lovely long black hair, and he is rotund and wonderfully jolly, and we all hit it off immediately, and spend a pleasant hour talking and watching the waiters fight.

Back on board *Star Flyer*, as we dress for dinner, we agree to look out for the Brazilians and sit with them, but when we get down to the dining room, to our absolute horror they are sitting with the scrap metal merchants, and the four of them, squeezed intimately into a side booth, are laughing and joking as though they have known each other for a lifetime.

'It is us. We aren't friendly enough,' I say to Geoffrey as we take a seat at an empty long table for eight, trying to ignore the joyful shrieks coming from their table. We feel like lepers as we look up hopefully at every couple that enters the dining room, willing them to join us. But it seems everyone this night has teamed up with like-minded people and they are all out to get to know and love each other. As each couple comes in, they look around the dining room, their eyes quickly glancing over us, see someone they have already bonded with, wave cheerfully and go and join them. There isn't even a sign of our gay Belgium couple. Even a depressing conversation about Europe going to the dogs is a merry prospect at the moment.

'We're losers,' I say as the laughter rises all around us and we struggle alone through our soup and entrée courses. Then finally the maître d' brings a good-looking young couple over and asks if they can join us.

'Sit,' I demand. 'Welcome. I love you.'

They look at me as though I have a weekend leave pass from the local mental hospital.

They are French. They do not—*will not*—speak English. And it is obvious that they strongly resent my asking if they do.

'*Non,*' says the girl, looking at me sharply as though I am a cockroach she has just discovered in her bouillabaisse.

The four of us are squashed at one end of the long table for eight. It is the most awkward, awful, anguishing meal I have ever sat through. I try to dredge up every bit of schoolgirl French I can remember but this woman is having none of it. Her husband tries, and even offers a welcome number of '*oui, oui, ouis*' to my many shrill questions, but it is hopeless. Then they ignore us completely and talk to each other in quiet French whispers. The laughter gets even louder at the scrap metal merchants' table and their voices carry easily to us.

'Is this great tucker or what?' comes the Aussie twang. 'We've had a bonza day in Rhodes. Busy though, flat out like lizards drinking.'

What the Brazilians make of that we can only guess, but they sure seem to be enjoying it all.

During the main course I am so uncomfortable I get up and go the ladies room. I stare in the mirror for as long as I decently can, hoping everyone will have finished and be gone by the time I get back, but no, they're French, and they're having every course, including a selection of five cheeses.

God, it's awful. I finally nudge Geoffrey—who has ploughed happily through his food as though nothing is amiss—to get him to leave, and we go upstairs towards the Tropical Bar, me in a lather of sweat. The scrap metal merchants' laughter follows us all the way up to the deck.

Greek dancers come on board to entertain us before we sail at midnight. The dancing is led by a papa with his three daughters and one son. It is very touristy but also very good, because of the papa. He is a short chubby man but incredibly light on his feet as he performs the elaborate steps, dipping and linking arms with the others and doing a number of traditional dances from the different islands, including Sifnos. The dances all look the same to me, but obviously there are subtle differences. His nice-looking daughters in traditional costume are delightful, and so is the young man, but it is papa who steals the show with his showmanship and urgings to the crowd to clap along with him. Naturally the performance ends with a rousing rendition of 'Zorba', and papa makes sure every passenger joins in. As is often the case with these things, you automatically decline to join in, thinking it is supremely nerdy, and you hold back, preferring to watch and keep on sipping on your wine at the bar, but when you finally do get involved and tumble excitedly around with everyone, it is tremendous fun.

By now the Brazilians and the scrap metal merchants have come up to the deck and are huddled at the bar, still laughing, sharing jokes and drinks and slapping backs. I can't stand it.

Papa finishes off the dancing by spinning himself into a frenzy that would make a dervish envious and then staggers off the ship, supported by his daughters. There is no alternative now but for us to retire, because I cannot tolerate the warm and heartfelt friendship that has sprung up between outback Australians and groovy Brazilians.

You might scoff at the thought of me being so envious of other people laughing together—and you're allowed to.

LOST IN A CASTLE
IN TURKEY

In Bodrum in Turkey our guide's name is Orchin and he's going to show us the famous St Peter's Castle, just a short walk from the port. We are standing outside its handsome walls now, looking at the surrounding yacht-filled harbour and feeling impressed.

'Bodrum is the St Tropez of Turkey,' Orchin says, and we can see this is indeed a glamorous place. The people are as attractive as the stylish white bougainvillea-clad houses dotting the surrounding hills, and the harbourside restaurants all look inviting and expensive.

Bodrum is a city in the southwest of Turkey, founded by the Dorians and conquered by the Persians in the fifth century BC. But I don't think anyone sitting in the cafés or on the yachts or by the pools at the water-front hotels cares much about that right now. Their brown oiled bodies in colourful bikinis and tiny swimsuits flop on lounge chairs and it is obvious that they are here just for the sun and the sea and the nightlife. I, however, am listening to Orchin. When Bodrum freed itself from

Persian rule, it became the capital of the independent province of Caria and the seat of the Carian kings, the most famous of whom was Mausolus. He was commemorated with a tomb called the Mausoleum, which is one of the Seven Wonders of the World. The Greek historians Herodotus and Dionysius of Halicarnassus were born in the city.

But no matter how interesting Orchin tries to make it all sound, people in our group appear more interested in the lively surrounds than in Greek historians, so he takes us inside the Castle of St Peter.

Its origins date back to the Knights of St John (my, but those boys got around). They came to Turkey in the fifteenth century and began work on the castle. The fortress became known as the Castle of St Peter the Liberator, and it served as the sole place of refuge for all Christians on the west coast of Asia during the time of the crusades. For over a century the castle was a stronghold for the knights. Under Turkish care it has had several uses, including as a military base, a prison and a public bath. Now it is a museum—and a lucrative tourist attraction, judging by the number of tourist groups about to enter its ancient walls.

The castle is also the home of the world's only Museum of Underwater Archaeology. That doesn't mean we have to don diving suits to look at works in the museum; it means it contains hundreds of items found and salvaged from wrecks beneath the water, ships that sank a long long time ago, one of them thirty-two centuries ago. How about that?

There are only about a dozen in our group with Orchin, and we wander through the castle's neat grounds admiring murals depicting life in the fifteenth century, all of us pondering our various thoughts— mine centring on how difficult ordinary life must have been then. I'm looking at a mural showing people trying to make olive oil, and it looks bloody hard work. One man pulls down on a tree branch with another man hanging from it, to press his weight on a basket of olives beneath slabs of stone. Another mural shows a couple of men in a tub frantically crushing olives.

'Just getting a meal on the table must have been such hard work back then,' I say to a woman near me.

'Yes, and your life expectancy was only around thirty,' she answers, and we both think about that for a minute.

'And your teeth used to rot at a very early age,' I say, knowing that they didn't realise the importance of oral hygiene back then. The woman doesn't answer me, but I can see she's enlightened. We continue, following Orchin, who is giving us so much historic detail, so many dates and so much talk of those busy Knights of St John that nobody can pay attention any more. But the underwater museum really does fascinate me. It has a replica of one of the ships that used to carry the olive oil to foreign parts, and I can tell you, those poor sailors lived and worked in the smallest of quarters. Just looking at the tiny galley down below sea level—it's no bigger than an Aussie outdoor dunny—brings me out in goose bumps. I spend a long time examining the exquisite glass salvaged from ships wrecked thousands of years ago. There are small, delicate blue and green glass jars, perfume bottles and dishes that could have been blown by one of our talented glass artists of today; they are so fascinating I don't realise the group has all gone on without me. Only Geoffrey remains.

It is not a pleasant feeling to have your group take off without you. Not because we are in the remotest bit of danger, apart from being fleeced by a souvenir seller in this tourist hive, but because no-one in the group has noticed our absence. It makes me think for a chilling moment about what that American couple, Tom and Eileen Lonergan, might have felt on the Barrier Reef when they surfaced after their dive to find that the boat had departed without them. Unimaginable.

'I was really enjoying all the information Orchin gave us,' I tell Geoffrey, who is searching the castle ground with his eyes for our group.

'So was I.'

'Worse, we've already paid for this tour. Let's find them.'

So we rush off down paths, over lawns, bypassing cannons, peering around towers, looking into dungeons and poking our heads into museums. There is no sign of them. We are pretty annoyed and join another group, but the leader—an observant man, unlike ours—notices two beefy strangers in his group and orders us away.

'You'll catch up with your own group in the English Tower,' he says.

English Tower? Why would a castle in Turkey have an English Tower, for goodness sake? But it does and we rush to it, anxious now, like lost and frightened children. There is still no sign of them. (But the English Tower is very English, if you're interested.) We run now through the castle grounds and finally spot our group up on another level, laughing and joking—and yes, the scrap metal merchants are there, booming about this being better than a poke in the eye with a burnt stick, and examining turrets and generally bonding with more fellow passengers. We wave to the group and call out to them but they ignore us. They take photos of each other against the backdrop of the castle. We have never felt so left out.

We try to reach them by a set of steep steps, but every time we get close they move on to another spot on another level, just out of our reach. We spend half the morning running in search of them, and feel miffed and abandoned. By the time we catch up with them the tour is over, and Orchin, who still has not noticed that we are not with him, tells everyone to go off to the bazaar next door and spend money.

'Turkey needs your tourist money,' he says. 'The war, Bush, not enough tourists. Please be kind to us.'

Well, you weren't so kind to us, Orchin, but we do go into the bazaar and spend our time, but not our money, strolling the narrow streets jammed with shops and cafés and tourists, and we really do enjoy the atmosphere. Jewellery is the big item for sale in Bodrum. Every shop is packed with gold and silver but there are not many customers buying anything. We head for a stall selling 'genuine fake watches' and bargain with a friendly man for a watch, but he says he cannot lower his price, because 'the war, Bush, no tourists', so we move on.

Back on board *Star Flyer* we pass on the origami and fruit-carving lessons (I know I told you *Star Flyer* was about a more elegant style of sailing, but hey, some things are just too damn traditional not to include on a cruise) and rest before dinner, determined this evening to sit with jovial people and laugh loudly in the direction of the scrap metal merchants. We ask the maître d' to sit us with someone this evening instead of taking an empty table ourselves, and he puts us with an attractive young couple from Belgium. We like them immediately, maybe because they are so interested in us and ask a lot of questions about Australia. Another middle-aged American couple come into the dining room and our new best Belgian friends wave vigorously at them to join us.

'How come you know so many people on board already?' I ask of the young Belgian man. 'We haven't got to know anybody yet. People haven't wanted to sit with us.'

'Well, you *are* big and intimidating,' he says, and beckons his American friends over. So there you go. With these few blunt words he has just explained away all the startled and frightened looks we receive from hotel receptionists and goats. All those people who jump back, raise their eyebrows, stare at us with undisguised fright have obviously been intimidated by our size.

'Big and intimidating?' I repeat, amazed. Big, yes, I have to accept that. But intimidating? Never.

He is fraught with remorse over my distress, realising his gaffe, and tries to make amends.

'I don't mean big as in fat, I mean big as in slender … you know what I mean … big … intimidating.'

By now the Americans have joined us and save us all from further embarrassment. Fortunately, they are charmed by our Australian accents and immediately ask us if we know a friend of theirs who lives in Wagga Wagga.

'We do not even know where Wagga Wagga is,' we tell them, which doesn't faze them at all.

'We met him on board this ship on a cruise a year ago,' they tell us. 'We became great friends; we love him to death. We love saying Wagga Wagga too. Are you sure you don't know where Wagga Wagga is?'

This prompts Geoffrey and me into discussing where it might be, because contrary to popular belief, not every Australian is intimate with the whereabouts of Wagga Wagga—although I am sure our scrap metal friends are. Neither of us can say for sure, and we agree to look it up in the atlas in the library tomorrow. The dinner continues with a reasonable amount of merriment, but not nearly as much as I would like to waft over to the scrap metal people, who are sitting yet again with the jolly Brazilians. (And I am still smarting from the 'big and intimidating' comments, so it's hard to be my usual vivacious and effervescent self.)

After dinner we go up to the Tropical Bar to watch the frog races. Now I know this little activity sounds like the ultimate in crassness, but I am here to tell you it is damn exciting. They are not real frogs, which disappoints us at first because we are Queenslanders, and while we may not know where Wagga Wagga is, we do know about cane toad races. But these are wooden frogs that are pulled along by a string over obstacles. The idea is for the onlookers to give as much ribald encouragement as possible while the frog-pullers hinder the other frog-pullers and generally cheat. Even the posh people who at first didn't want to get involved can't help but cheer raucously and shout coarse encouragement.

No-one can resist the simple kinds of entertainment on board these yachts. I remember last year, when we cruised on *Star Flyer* with our friends Ida and Jim Duncan. We were in the port of Livorno on the Italian coast when the crew put on their talent night and asked if any passengers had a special party piece they wanted to perform. Ida being Ida, immediately put her hand up and volunteered to recite some bush poetry. We were the only Australians on board, among French, Germans, Americans, Dutch, Norwegian and Belgian people, so I wasn't too sure how this would go down. But Ida would never let anything as unimportant as no-one understanding her get in the way of a good rendition of 'The Man from Snowy River'. So she started.

There was movement at the station, for the word had passed around
That the colt from old Regret had got away,
And had joined the wild bush horses—he was worth a thousand pound,
So all the cracks had gathered to the fray.

Although Ida recites well, and does all the voice inflections and hand movements, not a passenger on board, apart from Geoffrey, Jim Duncan and I had a clue what she was on about. But on she went, through another five verses, oblivious of the glazed-eye expressions all around her. And then, without any warning, a furious storm blew up from nowhere. Wind howled around the back deck at the Tropical Bar, sending glasses and bottles crashing off tables and bars, making the little flags strung around the decks flap noisily, sending chairs and bar stools into orbit.

Ida, with her hair streaming out behind her, clung to the piano and continued.

> So he went—they found the horses by the big mimosa clump—
> They raced away towards the mountain's brow,
> And the old man gave his orders, 'Boys, go at them from the jump,
> No use to try for fancy riding now.'

A champagne glass flew past Ida's ear. People struggled to open the doors to the safety of the decks below.

> So Clancy rode to wheel them—he was racing on the wing
> Where the best and boldest riders take their place,
> And he raced his stock-horse past them, and he made the ranges ring
> With the stockwhip, as he met them face to face.

There was no-one left at the Tropical Bar now but Geoffrey, Jim and me, holding onto the bar, surrounded by broken glass, upturned chairs and bar stools, abandoned jackets and activity programs.

> And where around the Overflow the reedbeds sweep and sway
> To the breezes, and the rolling plains are wide,
> The man from Snowy River is a household word today,
> And the stockmen tell the story of his ride.

Finally we managed to struggle against the wind towards Ida, grasp her in the safety of our arms and make our difficult way to the decks below.

'Where did everyone go?' she said.

Our tour this morning is led once again by Orchin. I still haven't told him off for forgetting us, but he is so nice that I hold my tongue as he takes us on board a small boat for a cruise down the Dalyan River. We have been told we can have a Turkish mud bath at the end of the cruise and everyone seems keener on the mud than on listening to details about the river or looking at the ancient tombs carved into the surrounding cliffs.

'By the time the archaeologists got to the tombs up there they had been robbed. Everything was taken,' Orchin says. *Yeah, a pity, but when do we get to the mud baths.*

He talks a lot about dates and the Persians attacking the Romans and somebody gaining independence by the second century.

'Very interesting,' I tell him. 'But will the mud ruin my new bathing suit or do we have to go naked?'

Fortunately for the other people on the tour, we do not have to go naked and the mud does not ruin bathing suits.

It is super slippery in the big mud hole and I am not the only one having trouble getting in, and not the only one looking like a big hippo on the banks of a lazy African river. The idea is to cover yourself in the warm mud, get out, let it dry, then shower it off, and have your skin glow with cleanliness. I once paid $100 for a small tube of such mud, and it really did leave the skin feeling clean and glowing, so I am all for this mud wallowing. People of all shapes and sizes are stepping cautiously into the mud. They're nervous at first, but once they're in, sitting down and smoothing big handfuls of the squelchy stuff over arms and backs, they become kids. Some start throwing it, which is a bit much mud in the eye for me, so I stay well back and help coat Geoffrey's considerable bulk with the slimy green stuff. Within ten minutes Geoffrey no longer resembles a human being. He looks very similar to the Incredible Hulk, as he is covered from the top of his balding head to the end of his fat toes. He looks so hideous that he becomes an attraction. All around us, people—not looking too attractive themselves, I have to tell you—have stopped to stare at him. He looks like something that has been exhumed. Only his teeth and the whites of his eyes are visible. Children cry and turn their faces to their mother's breasts.

We squelch our way out of the mud to stand in the sun so that it can dry. By now it is impossible to tell the men from the women. We are all sexless green creatures. The scene is so surreal you could be forgiven for thinking we are Aborigines at a corroboree—especially with the background of brown hills, huts and dusty fields. Someone (something?) comes up to me, gingerly hands me a camera and asks me to take a photo of them. I do, and then I discover that it is the scrap metal lady. I'm mortified that I hadn't recognised her. We stand together in the sun and talk. It is the first time I have spoken to her since that first night and I feel guilty, because she really is quite nice.

'I am worried about what to wear to dinner tonight,' she says. 'I am not one for bunging it on.'

'Why are you worried? It's casual dress,' I tell her. 'Just the same as last night.' *Star Flyer* has a casual dress policy and we all appreciate it.

'I know. It's just that we've bloody well been invited to sit at the Captain's table for a special dinner tonight and I'm so nervous I've got the collywobbles.'

I'm speechless. For all of my seafaring days I wanted to sit at the Captain's table but never ranked importantly enough, and now here my scrap metal beauty is offered the ultimate onboard privilege … *and I ran away from her after that first night.*

The mud takes forever to wash off in the communal showers. Dozens of us stand in eerie lines beneath the showers washing, scrubbing, rubbing until we glow pink. Much later, back on board *Star Flyer*, when I visit the loo I discover little flakes of dried mud in my knickers. It has got into dark places that are best not talked about … so I won't.

Finally, we have a really good time at dinner. While the scrap metal people sit formal and frightened at the Captain's table we get together with the Brazilians and a German couple and well, I can tell you, we just about all peed ourselves laughing.

Toby, the German man, has been on board for two weeks, and says he is alarmed at the large number of Americans on board this week.

'I really don't mind Americans, but they are loud,' he says. 'We had hardly any Americans last week. But we did have one couple, Bob and Nora. Bob was about 150 kilos and Nora wasn't far behind. Bob was a surgeon, but I don't know how he operated—he must have had his arms way out in front of him.'

Then Toby tells us about being pulled along on the long yellow banana boat—one of those big inflatable beach toys that half-a-dozen people sit on and get towed at great speed behind a boat—with Nora during the water sports in one of the ports. His story is so funny we roar with laughter and everyone at the Captain's table turns to stare enviously at us.

'Nora fell off the banana boat and nobody could get her back on,' Toby says. 'We all got in the water to try and heave her up. It took about three of us, and finally we got her on, and then she slipped right over the other side. It was hard enough because of her size, but she was covered in suntan oil as well. The water sports guys tried to get her on the back of their boat instead, and they got her halfway up, and then she was there like a beached whale. You have never seen people eat as much food as Bob and Nora. They even set their alarm clock so they could get up for the midnight snacks up on deck.' Toby's story was funny because the hapless Bob and Nora had long departed—we wouldn't have laughed so much if they'd still been on board. But I think you had to be there, hear Toby tell it himself with all the appropriate gesticulating. It doesn't sound so funny here in print.

And Wagga Wagga is in southwest New South Wales, by the way.

SANTORINI ...
BEAUTIFUL SANTORINI

Santorini. What can I say about this dazzling place that could do it justice? Is it *the* most romantic and picturesque place on earth? Certainly its image is known throughout the world. The blue-domed, white-washed buildings, the narrow stepped streets, the terraces packed with hotels, bars and restaurants, and the magnificent views to the brilliant Aegean have formed the backdrop for countless movies and glamorous photo shoots. From a distance, the clusters of white villages clinging to tall volcanic cliffs rising powerfully out of the Aegean Sea look like smears of white icing dripping down the dark volcanic mountains. This scene sends shivers down our backs, and no doubt down the backs of the millions of visitors sailing into Santorini on the ferries and cruise ships each summer.

Santorini is probably the most popular of all the Greek islands after Mykonos, and its outrageous hotel and restaurant prices reflect its appeal. It is hedonistic and decadent, and a destination to dream about on boring winter nights at home, but it also has a long and fascinating history and archaeological sites aplenty, some of which can prove that the first man present on the island dates back to the Neolithic Period. It also has the exciting Legend of Atlantis—the famous underwater city. Many tour guides will tell you it is not myth but truth, and it is satisfying to think so, even if you know you are kidding yourself. Santorini was colonised by the Minoans in 3000 BC, and gained its crescent shape after the volcanic eruption in 1450 BC.

It is part of the Cylades Islands cluster and lies in the heart of the Aegean. It enjoys long, hot, dry summers and colourful and extravagant sunsets. No-one can resist the romantic lure of Santorini. No-one can fail to be seduced.

We were here eight years ago, staying in the scenic village of Oia at the northern end of the island for a few weeks, blowing our entire year's holiday budget on accommodation in the windmill building— now a hotel—that overlooks the caldera and is featured on almost every brochure and postcard of Santorini. Our accommodation was a small two-bedroom cave-like apartment at the bottom of the windmill. It had a miniature fenced patio at the front, on which we sat for hours over coffee each morning, gazing dazedly down to the shimmering sea and across to the white-dotted mountain, certain we had stepped into a preposterously beautiful dream.

Oia is about twenty minutes from the main town of Fira, via a thrilling bus ride around hairpin bends on top of the cliffs, and is famous for being an excellent position from which to view the lingering sun as it sinks slowly behind the caldera. We probably had the best location of all to watch the sunset from our patio, but unfortunately, everyone else on the island thought so too. Each evening as the bars, restaurants and cafés put on the happy hour drinks and the haunting sunset music, out came the crowds. Thousands of people clogged the tight streets looking for anything to sit on—a wall, a rock, a bench, my patio chair—anything to enable them to stare blissfully for the three or so hours of stunning sunset. If you can imagine the big red ball of sun slowly sinking to the sea turning the water to liquid gold and streaking the sky with vivid reds, burnt orange, deep blues and dramatic purples, so that you feel as though you are sitting in the middle of an artist's palette of shimmering colour, then you may have some idea of the beauty of a Santorini sunset. So who could blame so many people for flocking and sitting enthralled on walls all over Oia for hours each evening? But why did they all want to sit on the stone wall of our patio—and yes, truly, some actually did come in through our tiny blue wooden gate to our patio and take up a chair by our table. It almost drove us to insanity.

Oia's tiny paved alleyways are actually its main streets, and although they are without traffic, they are still public streets, so the metre-wide strip outside our gate—all that stood between us and a sheer drop of many hundreds of metres to the sea below—was actually a public street, leading to a dead end right by our door. Hordes of people flocked by incessantly each night, and when they realised this was as far as they could go, they would plonk themselves down on our low wall. We would politely point out to them that this was private property, which we were paying hundreds of dollars a night for, and ask them nicely to leave. They would huff off angrily, only to be instantly replaced by a swarm of other flockers. Each night when we should have been mellowed to romance by the sunset, we were distracted to delirium by the flockers. This went on every evening until Geoffrey erected a temporary barricade of a propped-up deckchair across the 'road', just before our patio. This put off the first five hundred people, but the next thousand realised it was but a flimsy and unauthorised blockade; they removed it, and flocked once again …

But that was eight years ago. Now we revisit Oia and walk happily through its charming streets to our windmill place, just for a nostalgic look. And there, right where Geoffrey had made his insubstantial barricade, the owners have built a low but fearsomely solid concrete wall.

'Why, oh why hadn't they thought of that when we were here before?' we say, and take photos of the wall and the windmill and the backdrop of blue sea. We stand for half an hour staring dreamily at the scene, remembering the allure of our accommodation in the windmill, spoilt only by the evening flockers, and then Geoffrey goes inside the windmill to tell the hotel owners that we had stayed there eight years ago, and they get excited and look back through their guest book and find our names still there, and everyone seems thrilled by this simple encounter—except me—I am waiting outside, ready to explore Oia.

It is quiet this afternoon, and we have an uneasy feeling of disappointment. Oia seems to be waiting for something to happen. Maybe it is just siesta time, or maybe we're here before the really busy season, but the place seems unnaturally quiet. We walk up small streets, peer into empty jewellery shops, vacant art galleries and unfilled cafés, and then gaze out over low walls to the surrounding cliffs and down to the sea. We walk down steep steps and up gentle slopes, around slim corners and then down small steps and up high paths. That is how you must walk in the terraced maze of Santorini. We look down to whitewashed villas hanging over the edge of cliffs with pools that seem to be floating in the air, and we wonder what it must be like to swim in there, to lean against the edge and look up to the clear sky, down to the sheer drop. We ramble all over Oia, trying—and failing—to capture the romance. We even stop by a low wall, take photos and sigh sadly at the few colours—pale pinks, mauves and yellows—creeping into the once all white and blue domed landscape, and then use our mobile phone to telephone our daughter in Cairns in Australia just to tell her we are here. We describe the scene to her and she squeals with excitement, but we still cannot catch the strong feeling of awe we experienced eight years ago.

'Perhaps it's not a good thing to come back to a place you so loved and have such starry-eyed memories of,' Geoffrey says.

'Yes, such beautiful memories—apart from the flockers.'

'Once you've stayed in a place and enjoyed it so much, maybe it is best never to return. It just doesn't seem as enchanting this time.'

He is right. How well I remember our wide-eyed wonder as we sat in small cafés jutting out over the edge of cliffs, only to see a more appealing café below us in the distance. I recall the thrill of rushing through the white-walled streets the next day tracking down that better café for frappe and baklava, sitting in yet another dream location, then looking up to the cliffs and finding an even better positioned café. Every spot on the white dotted cliffs held magic and allure.

Each evening brought a confusion of choices. We would sit in a small bar and look out to Oia at night, a mass of twinkling lights in the white buildings. We would see other precariously positioned bars and restaurants overhanging the cliffs.

'Let's try to find that one,' we would say. We'd finish our drinks and rush off through the labyrinth searching for that elusive place, only to stumble across another exhilarating find in another higher or lower narrow street.

'This one will do' we would say at each place, tumbling in to sit and stare across the glitter of lights, impatiently finishing our drinks so we could once again sally forth and find that even more engaging café just over there and up and out a bit, suspended in blue space among the flicker of lights—or were they stars? And so it went every night. While it sometimes didn't make for relaxed dining, it certainly made us get around to most of the beautiful spots to dine on the island.

While it was a giddy and marvellous thing to be so high and look down on the measureless blue ocean, it was hot and there was no pool in our accommodation, so a swim, despite the considerable effort to get down the mountain, was tempting. We walked one day down the hundreds of steps to the Ammoudi Harbour. That day is as clear in my mind as the crystal water we swam in. Wandering past the tiny harbourside tavernas with their primitive barbecues outside—grids over hot coals—and scrambling awkwardly on the rocks, climbing over semi-naked people sunning themselves in every available spot, is still a vivid memory.

That was the first time that I had swum in the transparent Aegean waters for thirty years, and the feeling of bliss as the cool water slicked over my hot skin is as strong and as thrilling a memory as I have of anything in all my travels. After that swim, sitting in one of the harbourside taverns watching the fish I had chosen back in the kitchen being grilled on the hot coals, with my skin still cool and tingling from the heavenly water, I remember being as close to happiness as anyone would dare dream to be. And after the donkey ride back up the hundreds of steps, when the donkey man waived the charge because we didn't have the right change, I can recall thinking how lucky we are to have Greeks and Greece in the world.

Now, after our disappointment this time in Oia—alleviated a little by the excitement at the lack of stray dogs and corresponding dog poop on the streets, both of which had been so prominent before ('Greeks have cleaned up their act; they've finally realised the importance of tourism,' Geoffrey pontificates)—we take the bus back to Fira, itself a picturesque and mostly pedestrianised town perched on the cliffs. It is more commercial than Oia: the big cruise ships anchor in the port of Skala Firon 270 metres below and pour forth thousands of tourists—myself and Geoffrey included—every day in the height of the season.

In Fira, it seems everyone is a jeweller. Sumptuous jewellery shops sit side by side on every street, and I remind Geoffrey how fortunate he is to have a wife who isn't really interested in jewellery. I happen to think too much of it looks positively awful on a woman of a certain age. Older women have enough dangling bits without adding chains to their necks and chunky bracelets to their wrists. I am content with a small piece of black leather with a discreet bauble on the end of it around my neck, something that cost just a euro or two, but here in these glittering shops there are diamonds, rubies, pearls, sapphires and precious stones of every conceivable kind, all made into jewellery items of great flamboyance. We can imagine the trade these jewellers must do when the wealthy Germans and Americans spew out of the cruise ships, but today they have no customers despite there being a couple of ships in the harbour. All Mr Bush's fault, no doubt. The shopkeepers stand in doorways looking bored; they call out to each other, chatting, smoking, passing the time, making no sales.

We decide we have had enough of Santorini altogether, and walk down the long zigzag mule path of 580 steps to the harbour instead of taking the funicular. This turns out to be a huge mistake because it is steep, hot, pebbled and completely covered in donkey droppings. Boy, can those animals crap. It is impossible not to get our sandals and feet covered in the stuff, and we are quite distraught by the time we get to the bottom, way below. Our faces are burnt and ballooned, we sweat and stink, and then we get into a human traffic jam as a billion or so Americans clog the narrow steps at the bottom trying to get on the donkeys to take them up to the top. The heat, the crowd and the smell are overpowering, and they manage to banish any last remnant of warmth we feel towards Santorini. When we finally get free from the melée we head gratefully back on the tender boat to our *Star Flyer* home and drink three litre bottles of water. Later we sail off into the sunset with the sails unfurling and the bridge deck full of starry-eyed passengers who did get that first-time Santorini feeling.

At dinner we sit with the Brazilians and I ask them about the Greeks, because they have a Greek cousin who lives in Athens.

'Don't they get bored standing around in doorways all day, smoking and chatting to each other?' I ask.

'No, they have a coffee, talk, chat, it is the way of life. To them it is normal. They don't care about anything. They just like to talk to each other and pass the time.'

And that explains that. To me it sounds boring beyond endurance—a lifetime of just standing in doorways.

The Brazilians tell us about their lifestyle back in their home. He has his own business selling and installing elaborate video and DVD equipment into homes. They tell us how safe and fabulous Brazil is as long as you stay in the more affluent parts—theirs, we assume—and we are indeed tempted to put Brazil on our travel itinerary for another time.

This is our second-last night on board, and the scrap metal people have by now become best friends with almost every other passenger. They have lunched with Americans, taken afternoon tea with the attractive Belgian couple, shared cocktails with the French couple who refused to speak to us, danced with a young English couple, promised to visit the Canadians for skiing in the winter, sung 'Yes We Have No Bananas' with the Norwegians, and booked to go on another cruise next year with the Brazilians (and let's not forget that invitation to the Captain's table).

'It has to be us,' I comment to Geoffrey after dinner, as they pull up bar stools with our gay Belgian couple to discuss the decline of Europe. 'You need to be more friendly.'

Tonight we watch another talent show by the crew, and Ramon our Filipino barman does a raunchy Ricky Martin number, complete with swivelling hips and huge smile. He makes everyone feel so good just watching him that we all get up and gyrate our hips for a while—and look like a big bunch of cruise geeks. Then we listen to sea shanties by the rest of the crew and watch a spot of Greek dancing, with some really woeful audience participation. It ends with all of us doing the Macarena … and yes, I know exactly what you are thinking—what a bunch of losers—but if you were here, you'd do it too. You simply cannot help getting into the spirit of it, whether you are old or young—and the really amazing thing this night is that no-one seems to be drunk.

When we retire to our cabin and I am massaging my gums in the tiny bathroom, I look at the small toilet and think I am just about ready to finish with this travelling and get back to Australia. When you start yearning for your own toilet, you know it is time to go home. Don't laugh; your own toilet is beautiful thing. Your familiarity with it, your comfort and confidence while perched on it, is something to be cherished. I bet you have never given this a thought before—I am glad I brought it to your attention.

So, what else do I miss about home? I mentally compose a list.

My electric toothbrush. These hand jobs just do not massage gums nearly well enough for a gum fanatic such as myself.

Routines. I miss the routine of my morning walk in the park, the sound of kookaburras calling to each other in the early morning. I miss the moist forest smell of the park.

Work. Yes. Believe it. Some people really do need to work to be fulfilled, and I am one of them.

My supermarket, and the intimate knowledge I have of it. I could go around the aisles with a blindfold choosing my products if I had to.

English-speaking voices all around me.

My spacious shower. (Our shower at home is exceptionally big, not because we are rich, but because there was an awkward big space in a corner when the bathroom planner drew up his plans, so he made the shower into a mini ballroom—I could shower and hold a cocktail party in there at the same time. And I'd invite you around but I know you wouldn't come.)

My three offspring.

My few mates.

My kitchen. No more trying to make a tomato sandwich on the bedside table, although it has been interesting trying to be culinarily creative in hotel rooms. I once interviewed the delightfully eccentric English-turned-Aussie chef, Ian Parmenter (I do like to drop these names, don't I?), and he talked about his own travels and how he tired of restaurant meals. He gave a demonstration of how you could cook yourself a multi-course dinner in your hotel room. He actually ironed a veal steak to tender perfection between two sheets of greaseproof paper, boiled a corncob in the kettle, and heated up baked beans with the hair dryer. I liked that, but unfortunately, most Greek hotels don't have hair dryers, kettles or irons.

I also miss the Australian television news presenters.

And I'd kill for a glass of good Domain Chandon bubbles.

And a bottle of Rosemount Cab Sav.

I really do miss the myriad food choices in Australia. Indian tonight, love? No, Thai perhaps. Nup, I'm in the mood for Malaysian, or maybe a Chinese takeaway, but then again I could go Italian. It's all there, every cuisine a person could ask for.

And may no-one ever present a Greek salad to me again.

THE END HAS TO COME

We spent our last day of the cruise on the island of Hydra, a small island just a 45-minute ferry ride from Athens. I had not heard of it, and didn't have much interest in it—I was completely focused on getting home to my toilet and electric toothbrush. Well, wasn't I the foolish one? It turns out to be a most captivating small island with a little bit of Italy in its back streets and a lot of Monte Carlo in its harbour. We didn't discover all this enchantment until the afternoon. We spent the morning lazing on the beach around the bay from Hydra's port, away from all the main activities, with me ogling the Swedish water sports guys. They had brought the banana boat over to the beach and were giving the teenagers frantic zooms around the bay. I was very tempted to have a go myself, but the bronzed Swedes deliberately tip it over to heighten the experience—everyone falls off and shrieks with laughter, and it's all part of the thrill—but I know I would be another Nora trying to get back up on that big yellow thing. Instead I listen in on the conversation of a Norwegian mother and her young son sitting nearby. I can't think of another language that spurts out at such speed. It doesn't even sound like a language; it's more a slur of sloshing noises. The two of them talk to each other all morning, and seem to be involved in an erudite discussion, even though the boy is all of ten.

We return to the ship and are propping ourselves up at the bar, guzzling as much champagne as we can fit in before the end of the cruise, when the gay Belgian couple come running up to us saying we have to get back ashore to see the charm of Hydra.

'It's gorgeous, like Mykonos, no, like Italy, no … I don't know, it's just beautiful.'

We reluctantly leave our champagne and get on the tender and head ashore again. And I am very glad we do.

No cars, not even scooters are allowed on this island. The only mode of transport is the donkey. The town centres around a small but picturesque harbour crammed with lavish yachts, with well-fed people sitting on their spacious back decks. All around the harbour are the wicker chairs and tables of the cafés and tavernas, and the docile donkeys move between them with packs of supermarket supplies on their backs, walking up from the harbour to the back streets to deliver their goods. The Greeks on this island have planted the bougainvillea everywhere, and it blooms bright and purple at every turn. It grows up whitewashed walls, out of terracotta tubs and over trellises to hang colourfully over small restaurants in the beautiful squares. We follow a donkey carrying a heavy load of bottled water and boxes of other goods to a tiny supermarket, which looks like no more than a hole in the wall. We pass boutique hotels and peek into reception areas of abundant marble, and walk by open windows where the smell of ubiquitous hotel soap wafts out on the air. We get pleasantly lost in the confusion of streets and pop out to more shady small squares, some completely covered in grapevines, where proprietors are getting their restaurants ready for the evening rush. It is a tourist haven, but who cares?

Most of the buildings are whitewashed, some are of the same stone we saw everywhere in Lesbos, some have Italian-style shutters … it is all captivating.

'I could spend weeks here,' Geoffrey says, and I'm with him on that one. Most travellers scorn these tourist hot spots, but to me they have enormous appeal. Maybe because I enjoy sitting in busy cafés looking at rich people at play—but only in small doses as I soon tire of being in crowded places.

Which is what we do when we head back to the harbour and take chairs one of the hundred or so tables around the water.

'Why do rich people on yachts always have big girths?' Geoffrey asks as one particularly large man, naked to the waist, sits on a long chair on the deck of his yacht staring at us while we stare at him.

'Because they can, I suppose. You would too if you could eat and drink all day long, every day of the year. And our girths aren't exactly wispy.'

This unpleasant thought shuts us up for a while as we both look down at our protruding stomachs. We had endeavoured to trim down before we left Australia, knowing that one always puts on considerable weight on a long holiday. But we had failed to lose even a kilo before we left, and now we have bloated out beyond recognition. I particularly dread going back to work—colleagues are sure to gasp in shock as I waddle in the door.

For our last dinner on board we try not to look enviously at the scrap metal people, and to enjoy the company of the groovy Belgian couple (not the gay ones). We listen to them telling us how much they disliked Hydra because of its commercialism.

'It is awful. We don't like these places at all,' the groovy guy says.

'I love them,' I reply.

'No, the Greek islands are spoilt forever now with all the tourists.'

Yeah, and you are one of them, I want to say, but I refrain, because they are our only friends on board.

In the morning we watch the scrap metallers embrace and kiss every other passenger, saying tearful goodbyes, offering invites to outback Queensland and promising to visit new friends all over the world. They give us a reluctant handshake, say they are in a hurry to catch a plane and have to shoot through like a Bondi tram, and I want to shout after them: 'Come back, be our friends, we're sorry we initially judged you.'

As everyone else hugs newly made friends, Geoffrey and I make our lonely way to the bus that will take us into Athens.

'What's wrong with us?' I ask him.

'We are big and intimidating.'

We have one more day in Athens before our flight back. It is much hotter now than it was when we were here at the start of our holiday, months before. We stay in another cheap hotel where the room is smaller than my laundry room at home and the bathroom is so cramped my knees scrape the wall as I sit on the loo. But it is air-conditioned and it does have a rooftop garden with a stunning view over to the Acropolis, and we sit up there in the oppressive heat drinking warm beer and wine for as long as we can stand it. Then we go back to our room and flop on the bed to cool off and read the English papers.

The British government wants to make all overweight people sign a contract to lose weight before they will be given the benefits of the National Health system. This has caused outrage in fat people circles and smugness among the skinnies.

The cheating *Who Wants To Be A Millionaire?* couple have now gained celebrity status and are considering posing nude for *Playboy* magazine and going on the cover of *Mensa* magazine, because he— Major Charles Ingram—took an IQ test, and it proved he was fact quite intelligent as well as a cheat. And there is news of yet another reality television show, this time called *How Clean Is Your Home?*, where Britons search for the dirtiest house in the land, and one proud young mother in the paper today is claiming she could win because she has the deep fryer from hell. There you go. Don't say you never learn anything from me.

Bored with the papers, we turn on the little television sitting high on the wall on a bracket and watch CNN for an hour. On comes an item about surveys of the habits of people of various cultures; there is also a survey of the most desirable places to live in the world. Oslo, in Norway, comes in at number one.

'But don't these survey people know they sing crappy songs in Norway?' I ask Geoffrey, who says, 'Obviously they don't' and then tells me to be quiet because there, coming in at number four, is Australia.

'Living in one of the top five countries in the world for living standards is for me,' Geoffrey says, and we both get excited for a few minutes.

Greece comes in at number two on the survey for numbers of smokers. Japan is next. Iceland comes top on the empowerment of women. Yemen is on the bottom. Albania comes top in the bribery stakes. I really do learn something every day.

At night we wander listlessly around the Plaka, anxious now to leave. What seemed so vibrant and thrilling on the night we arrived now appears tiresome and annoying. Every restaurateur spruiks for business outside his café, thrusting business cards at us, urging us to return tomorrow night for the best food in Athens. But I am sick of oily moussaka, bored with tiny fried fish, fed up with eggplant dip, and wish never to see another olive, tomato, fetta and onion salad again. (I cannot even bring myself to say 'Greek salad' ... see what has happened to me?)

In the heat of the next morning we determine to visit all the museums we haven't seen before—our flight isn't until the evening, and as anxious as we are to get home, we simply cannot waste this last precious day in Athens.

'It's Saturday. The Archaeological Museum, the best and most beautiful one of all, is shut,' the hotel receptionist says with a brilliant smile.

'Wouldn't that rip your britches,' I say, because even though I hate her, I would really like to charm this person, probably one of the last foreign people I will see on this visit, and if it takes antiquated Aussie expressions to do it, then I am prepared to use them.

'Excuse me?' she says, looking bewildered.

'Wouldn't that rot your socks, stone the crows and make your bucket of prawns go off in the sun!' But what worked for scrap metallers just doesn't work for me: she takes several steps back, then gets out her map and points out one of the couple of museums open today. It takes us an age to find the Benaki Museum in Vasillissi Sofias Avenue, even though it is close to the metro stop. We walk along the fearsomely hot street, wandering for a cool air-conditioned minute into The War Museum to ask the receptionist where the hell the Benaki Museum is ... and, actually, what the hell is it? He directs us further up the road and finally we find it, in a graceful neoclassical building. It is heaven to step inside the cool hall and sink into one of the comfortable chairs in reception while Geoffrey pays for the entrance tickets, to unglue my skirt from my sweaty legs and catch my breath and comb the damp hair away from my face.

'We looked at many ancient and old things,' I have written, most articulately, in my notes. *Ancient and old things.* It must have been the heat, the stress, the mess of Athens. Surely?

Antonis Benakis is a bloke who was fortunate enough to be born into a distinguished and old family of the Greek diaspora that gave invaluable service to the political, social and cultural life of Greece. He founded the Benaki Museum in 1930. As soon as Benakis, who lived in Egypt, began to acquire his collection, he planned to donate it to the Greek state. His photograph—he was a handsome white-haired, white-moustached man—dominates the reception area, so visitors will always be sure it is him they have to thank for the amazing collection housed in this museum. The Greek public chipped in a bit to add to the collection and the museum continues to be the recipient of considerable material—complete collections of artworks as well as single masterpieces and more modest objects.

We spend a long time in the museum, going up and down its many levels several times. The thing I remember most from this hot and exhausting day of looking at countless precious objects of cultural significance is the gold snake bracelets and small gold earrings dug up from archaeological sites. They must be many thousands of years old yet they could perfectly well be worn today.

'How could anyone keep earrings for thousands of years when I lose mine after just one day?' I ask Geoffrey, who doesn't bother to answer because he is closely examining a tapestry depicting the raising of Lazarus.

On the top level there is a photographic exhibition of work by someone called Henri Cartier-Bresson, a Frenchman who was the father of photojournalism, apparently. We have paid extra to see this, and we wander along examining the large black and white photos of people and landscapes, but are furious to see that every caption gives a description in French only. Not one word of English (or Greek, for that matter) to explain to the larger audience what the pictures are. So, to the curators of the Henri Cartier-Bresson exhibition, whoever you are, a little bit of English (or indeed Greek) description would have made your exhibition something enjoyable instead of something puzzling. (Somehow, I doubt that little petulant show of objection would cut anyone to the quick, since it comes from a woman who writes *ancient and old things* and can only talk about gold earrings and snake bracelets after seeing a plethora of remarkable historical objects.)

On the bus to the airport this afternoon—a non-smoking air-conditioned bus costing just a beautiful three euros instead of a 60-euro taxi ride—we listen in to a particularly loud American couple talking to another American, a quiet dignified man who nods and listens silently. The American woman does not stop talking for one moment, but I like her loud voice and her traveller's tales of woe. She spent time in Italy before coming to Greece, and found everything wanting there. Not enough ice in the drinks, no air-conditioning in the bars, no proper French fries in the cafés, hard paper in the loos, the heat, the crowds, the inadequate plumbing. It has been the same in Athens—the Sprite and Diet Coke not cold enough, the funny lamb stews, the strange language, that dreadful no-paper-down-the-toilet thing.

We pass by messy roadworks and half-built stadiums, and the quiet man points out to her the work being done for the Olympics.

'Oh, are the Olympics here this year?' she asks loudly.

'No, next year.'

'Oh, I don't know where they are held from one year to the next,' she says dismissively, and I want to reach out and hug her tight because her strident and confident ignorance makes me think I am not such a hopeless ignoramus after all. I know I have not even begun to scrape the surface layer of Greece and its fascinating culture this summer. I haven't had the opportunity to be with these wonderful Greek people for any real length of time, and apart from my interviews with the wives on Sifnos and my all-too-brief encounters with a few restaurant and hotel owners, I haven't got to know any Greeks at all. But I have appreciated the colour and texture of Greek life, the pleasure of the sea, the beauty of the landscape, the history in the buildings, the pleasing rhythms of the villages. I have felt it all. I have loved it all. I have appreciated it all. I think I have seized the days. Well, the afternoons at least.

On the Qantas flight home they serve a Greek salad.

ABOUT THE AUTHOR

Born in the United Kingdom, Ann Rickard immigrated to Australia with her parents and spent her formative years in Melbourne before returning to England to live for ten years with her husband Geoffrey. After coming back to Australia they lived in Melbourne, raising their three children and then moved to Queensland in 1991 to live in Noosa. Ann is a full-time feature writer with the *Sunshine Coast Daily* as well as a travel author, and is slowly moving towards her goal of spending half her time in Australia, half in Europe. See Ann's slide show of the Greek islands at www.annrickard.com and contact her if you wish—she likes that.